GRESLEY and STANIER

1 & 2 The Settle & Carlisle line was opened in the year Gresley and Stanier were born. The most successful steam locomotives to work over this difficult route were the Class A3 and rebuilt Scot. These two views of 'The Thames–Clyde Express' show A3 60092 *Fairway* working the up train through Bingley and 6P 46109 *Royal Engineer* on the down train at Smardale. (1. W. Hubert Foster) (2. E.D. Bruton collection– NRM)

NATIONAL RAILWAY MUSEUM, YORK
PART OF THE SCIENCE MUSEUM, LONDON

GRESLEY and STANIER

JOHN BELLWOOD and DAVID JENKINSON

Sir Herbert Nigel Gresley

Sir William Arthur Stanier

LONDON   HER MAJESTY'S STATIONERY OFFICE

©Crown copyright 1986
First published 1976
Second edition 1986

ISBN 0 11 290438 6

CONTENTS

INTRODUCTION

Life is full of coincidences, and railways are no exception, but it was surely one of the more interesting tricks of fate that less than a month in the late spring of 1876 should separate the birth of the two men, William Arthur Stanier and Herbert Nigel Gresley, who were, over half a century later, to prove to be two of the most outstanding British locomotive engineers of the twentieth century. It was this coincidence of birth year, together with the planned arrival of Stanier's *Duchess of Hamilton* to join its Gresley contemporary *Mallard* in the National Railway Museum during their designers' centenary year, which provided the inspiration for this commemorative publication.

Wherever steam locomotives are discussed, then there will be people to argue their respective merits – and neither Gresley nor Stanier lack their apologists. It is, of course, too late now to affect the issue one way or the other; but that is unlikely to stop the debate. Nevertheless, we have tried to take an objective view, and what has struck us forcibly, in comparing the work of two fine engineers, is the amount of common ground between two men so outwardly different in approach and personality. One cannot help but feel that much of the so called rivalry between the two was probably more a reflection of the supporters and public relations departments of their respective railways than an indication of any real differences between the two engineers as men. They were, in fact, personal friends and it was Gresley himself, who in 1937, cheerfully accepted one of Stanier's lieutenants, Roland Bond, as nominee to take charge of the proposed LNER/LMS locomotive testing plant at Rugby.

The authors are unashamed admirers of the work of both these great engineers and we felt that their centenary should not go unmarked. If there is any prejudice, then at least it is equally divided between us. Others, better qualified, have already written more exhaustive technical accounts of their work. This book therefore, is no more than a simple comparison of the achievements and contributions of two note-worthy men, offered as a sincere and affectionate tribute to their memory.

This is the first book published by the National Railway Museum and we would like to thank our colleagues on the museum staff for their helpful encouragement and advice. In particular we are grateful for the finding and printing of many photographs and for the typing of the manuscript against a very tight deadline. All the illustrations used are from the Official Museum or BR collections except where acknowledged otherwise.

John Bellwood
Chief Mechanical Engineer

David Jenkinson
Head of Education and Research

National Railway Museum, York
May 1976

Introduction to the Second Edition

When "Gresley and Stanier" was written in 1976 it was intended to be no more than a tribute to the two engineers in the Centenary Year of their birth. However, many favourable comments were received and the 7000 copies printed soon sold out, to be followed by regular requests, from as far afield as Australia, for a reprint. Unfortunately this was not a straightforward operation as the photographic blocks were no longer available. It was therefore decided that, if there was to be a reprint, the opportunity would be taken to largely re-illustrate the original text and, perhaps, include some additional material.

The authors were most gratified to receive charming and appreciative letters from both Sir Nigel's and Sir William's daughters.

Communications were also received from a number of senior officers of the former LNER and LMS railways, who had worked with the respective, and obviously respected, CMEs. As a result our own knowledge and appreciation of the men and their work increased considerably. An account of how Stanier was finally persuaded to forsake the GWR for the LMS is probably not for general publication!

The Gresley and Stanier heritage has continued to be enjoyed by thousands of railway enthusiasts and students of locomotive, carriage and wagon practice and performance. In the intervening years since 1976, "Flying Scotsman" and "Sir Nigel Gresley" have probably been the LNER flagships, but by no means the only working examples of Gresley's enterprise. "Duchess of Hamilton" has been transformed from a static museum exhibit to a working traction unit again, regularly delighting hundreds of participants and lineside observers with impressive performances over the Settle and Carlisle line. Many other examples from the Stanier stable are very much a part of the independent railway preservation scene.

There is no substitute for first-hand experience. It is, however, hoped this second edition of "Gresley and Stanier" will help foster a continued interest in the work of the two eminent railway engineers and perhaps add some background appreciation to the sight of an elegant Gresley or majestic Stanier pacific in full cry on the main-line.

Once again, we would wish to record our appreciation of the help given by colleagues at the National Railway Museum, in particular John Edgington, who was largely responsible for unearthing the 'new' illustrations.

John Bellwood
Chief Mechanical Engineer

David Jenkinson
Head of Education and Research

National Railway Museum, York
April 1986

1

Two famous engineers

The year 1876 marks something of a watershed in British railway history. On 1st May that year the Midland railway inaugurated its own independent passenger services to Carlisle via Settle and, apart from the somewhat maverick Great Central Railway extension to London at the turn of the 19th and 20th centuries, the overall pattern of main line routes could be said to be complete. It is also true that some vital lines in the Scottish Highlands were still to be built, but in terms of high density routes, the main pattern was largely established and, in particular, there were now three rival routes to Scotland; East Coast, West Coast and Midland. It was on to this scene, only a few weeks later, that William Stanier was born on 27th May and Nigel Gresley on 19th June. Stanier was the son of a Wiltshire railwayman and Gresley the son of a Derbyshire clergyman whose ancestry stretched back to the Norman period.

One must beware of a temptation to stretch coincidence to the point of incredulity, but these closely spaced events in early 1876 were, to say the least, interesting in the light of subsequent railway history. The Midland Railway, with its new route, made an all-out assault on the travelling public in terms of improved comforts and facilities on its trains for even the humblest passenger. By admitting third class travellers to all trains, abolishing the second class and reducing first class fares to second class levels it created a minor revolution in passenger travel. Not only did this stimulate other routes to improve their facilities but it provided a very strong reason for its competitors to improve their journey times – for the Midland's route

offered much less of a threat in this field. Thus began an East/West Coast rivalry in matters of speed which has periodically broken out ever since, often in a quite spectacular manner, and to which Gresley and Stanier both fell heirs when steam locomotive development was in its prime.

Somehow it seemed entirely appropriate that in the final years of British steam trains, the finest products of Gresley's and Stanier's genius were to be seen working in harmony on that very same Midland route which, almost 100 years earlier, had been one of the causes which over the years helped to lead to their development.

Both Stanier and Gresley showed an early interest in railway engineering and each served his apprenticeship in the time honoured 19th century manner. Stanier not unnaturally went to the Swindon Works of the Great Western Railway, where he worked under such giants as William Dean and George Jackson Churchward; and for almost 40 years his allegiance was to one railway only, the GWR. Gresley, on the other hand, although he lived nearer to Derby, took up his apprenticeship at the famous Crewe works of the London & North Western Railway. At that time the reputation of Crewe was unrivalled and Gresley became a pupil under the autocratic F.W. Webb in 1893. It was the same Crewe Works that over 40 years later was to build some of the finest of Stanier's locomotive designs.

Gresley's subsequent rise through the railway hierarchy was rapid. He was a confident young man and immediately after completing his apprenticeship in 1898, moved to the Lancashire & Yorkshire Railway to gain design office experience under J.F. Aspinall, one of the greatest British locomotive engineers. Following a period in charge of the Horwich materials test room, Gresley was sent to Blackpool as foreman of the locomotive running shed. By 1901 he had been appointed as Assistant Works Manager of the LYR carriage works at Newton Heath and when he was only 28, he became Assistant Superintendent of the Carriage and Wagon Department.

That Gresley was ambitious cannot be denied, nor that he had his share of good fortune, but he was also shrewd. The LYR presented him with little further prospect of promotion since all its relevant senior appointments were held by relatively young men. Gresley therefore looked to a railway with an older Chief Mechanical Engineer and in 1905 moved to the East Coast route as Carriage and Wagon superintendent to the Great Northern

Railway under H.A. Ivatt. Ivatt himself had achieved considerable fame as a locomotive engineer and, by yet another of those strange coincidences, had also served at Crewe as an apprentice under F.W. Webb.

Gresley's and Ivatt's personalities were poles apart and one might have imagined the austere and cautious Ivatt viewing the activities of his confident young colleague with some misgiving. But the two men quickly developed a strong mutual regard for each other and Gresley soon became involved with improving the quality of the East Coast rolling stock, being particularly remembered for the characteristic bow-ended teak clad coaches which became a GNR and LNER trademark for more than 30 years.

It was no surprise when, on the retirement of Ivatt in 1911, Gresley was appointed as his successor on the Great Northern Railway at the relatively early age of 35. He had gained a wide

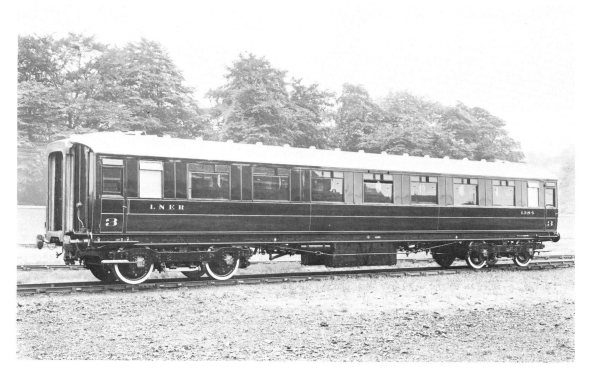

3 Standard Gresley teak bodied seven compartment side corridor coach No 1384 built at York in 1932 to Diagram 155.

4 Stirling 8-foot single No 1 built in 1870 was still in service when Gresley joined the GNR in 1905. Seventeen years later his Pacific *Great Northern* was to set the scene for East Coast main line motive power until the end of steam traction in the 1960s. Fortunately, through Gresley's personal intervention, No 1 is still with us; sadly his pioneer Pacific is not.

variety of experience of railway engineering and did not lack the confidence to proceed. So began the Gresley era when for 30 years he had charge first of the Great Northern Railway and later, after the 1923 grouping, of the much enlarged London & North Eastern Railway group. At first the LNER proposed to appoint J.G. Robinson of the Great Central Railway as the new CME, but he was near retirement and declined the offer, recommending Gresley for the job. Ironically, Robinson was to outlive the man for whom he stood aside.

Throughout the 1920s and 1930s Gresley's name was rarely far from the headlines in the railway world. His locomotives were graceful and speedy, they captured public imagination in a manner which few others approached and none surpassed and by the time his designs reached their zenith in the mid-1930s Gresley was a prime exponent of all the newly developing arts of the publicity men. Most of the early teething troubles, inevitably experienced with some new designs, had been overcome and such was Gresley's charisma, after such a long spell as CME, that it must have seemed to his men, particularly the footplate crews, that their

Chief could never go wrong. His knighthood in 1936 and his final triumph in 1938 when *Mallard* captured the world's steam speed record in resounding fashion, could only serve to reinforce this view. Consequently, when he died suddenly in 1941 after a heart attack, the whole of the railway world was stunned. He was only 64 and had probably driven himself even harder than the footplate crews drove his locomotives.

Gresley's reign thus came to an abrupt end and, regrettably, his successor Edward Thompson was not cast in the same mould. Wartime conditions would have forced some changes on the LNER and it is probable that Gresley himself would have seen the virtue of some of those which Thompson made; but it was the manner of them which probably caused most upset.Gresley's engines were thoroughbreds and although brilliant in concept, not perhaps ideally suited for the rough and tumble conditions of wartime operations and maintenance. Thompson recognised this and instituted some worthwhile changes, but often with little regard to the feelings of the men who would be most affected by them. At the same time it cannot be denied that some of Gresley's

5 The freight version of *Great Northern*, Class P1 2–8–2 No 2393 hauls a heavy up coal train through Sandy.
(G.H. Soole collection– NRM)

designs were less than trouble free during some critical wartime and early postwar years and perhaps in consequence were less influential in the choice of the British Railways standard designs than might have been expected.

The Gresley look remained part of the East Coast scene until the end of steam. The post-Gresley designs of Thompson, and particularly Peppercorn, shared many visual similarities to their predecessors, but they never quite seemed to possess the sheer panache of the great man's work. By the time better operating conditions had returned, Gresley's engines once more came into their own. Indeed, with the general adoption throughout the class of the modifications incorporated in *Humorist* in 1938, the A3 Pacifics were never better than in the late 1950s and early 1960s–quite a tribute to a basically 40 year old design–and, of course, no design ever approached the streamlined A4 as the supreme high-speed locomotive type.

If Gresley's rise to pre-eminence was meteoric and his fame unquestioned, Stanier's career was almost sluggish by comparison, though no less thorough in the grounding he received in railway engineering. The son of William Dean's chief clerk, Stanier began his railway life as an office boy at Swindon, actually starting his apprenticeship to Dean in May 1892. During that month, in one memorable weekend, the Great Western Railway converted all its residual broad gauge lines to standard gauge.

After his five year apprenticeship, Stanier worked his way via the GWR drawing office and the post of Inspector of Materials to the job of Locomotive Mechanical Inspector. No change of company for him–he was a GWR man to the core–but promotion came rapidly and by 1903, Stanier was an Assistant Divisional Superintendent at Westbourne Park. This was a significant period in locomotive history, for only a year earlier, George Jackson Churchward had taken over as Locomotive Carriage & Wagon Superintendent of the Great Western Railway. Churchward's influence on British locomotive design was immense and he almost certainly

6 Express passenger 2-8-2, P2 No 2003 *Lord President* leaving Edinburgh Waverley with an Aberdeen express.

merits the title of Britain's most outstanding steam locomotive engineer of the twentieth century. His work was the best part of a generation ahead of that to be found elsewhere and under these circumstances it is not surprising that most of his younger colleagues, including Stanier, probably felt that they had nothing to lose and everything to gain by remaining in Churchward's team. Events were to make Stanier into Churchward's most noteworthy disciple although it seems unlikely that at the time he could have ever realised this.

It is only fitting that Churchward's name should figure prominently in a tribute to Gresley and Stanier, for both men owed him much and Gresley said so publicly in 1936 at a meeting of the Institution of Locomotive Engineers: 'I was pleased to hear Mr Stanier refer to his old Chief, Mr Churchward, because I have always thought, and still think, that locomotive engineers in this country owe more to the ingenuity, inventiveness and foresight of Churchward than to any other Chief Mechanical Engineer. I know that his influence on the locomotives of this country still exists in a very marked way. Look at the latest locomotives of the Great Western, on the Southern, on the LMS, obviously, and also on the LNE. There is a great deal of Churchward's work which I was only too glad to incorporate on the engines of the London & North Eastern'.

The greatness of a locomotive engineer can often depend on the degree to which he is prepared to build on the work of eminent predecessors, and the fact that Gresley and Stanier were both prepared to learn from Churchward in no small way helps to explain why they too can be bracketed with him as Britain's foremost twentieth century locomotive engineers.

Stanier himself remained with the GWR during the whole of the Churchward years, becoming Divisional Locomotive Superintendent at Swindon in 1906, Assistant Works Manager at Swindon in 1913, Works Manager in 1920 and finally in 1923, Principal Assistant to Churchward's successor, C. B. Collett. By this time, Gresley had been a CME in his own right on the GNR for 12 years and was about to embark on his successful LNER career. Few if any people could then have imagined what was later to happen to William Stanier.

7 The up 'Silver Jubilee' and 10.00 am Newcastle–Liverpool express neck and neck on King Edward Bridge over the River Tyne. Class A4 No 2512 *Silver Fox* and A1 2582 *Sir Hugo*. (W.B. Greenfield)

Collett followed the Churchward traditions on the GWR which culminated in the production of Swindon's most impressive design, the famous 'King' Class 4-6-0. Stanier himself accompanied the pioneer member No 6000 *King George V* to the centenary celebrations in America of the Baltimore and Ohio Railroad in 1927, and there seemed no reason to suppose that he would not eventually succeed as CME to the Great Western Railway. However, like Gresley on the LYR over 20 years earlier, Stanier was too close in age to his seniors to have much hope of more than a short reign at the top, and on Britain's largest railway, the London Midland & Scottish, a motive power crisis was developing.

Alone of the four big companies at the 1923 grouping, the LMS locomotive department had undergone a more than difficult transition period to the new order. Gresley had been virtually unchallenged on the LNER after Robinson stood down, there was a general and widespread acceptance of Maunsell on the

Southern Railway and the GWR was so much bigger than the other railways in its group that it had merely absorbed them and retained its old title. But the LMS had problems.

This group drew together some of the most strong-minded and independent railway companies in the kingdom, in particular the London & North Western and the Midland Railways in England, together with their respective Scottish allies, the Caledonian and the Glasgow & South Western Railways. Each of these constituents had their strengths and weaknesses but there was never the same unity of interest as among the LNER constituents which mostly complemented each other up the East Coast of Britain; for the LMS had inherited two of the three rival routes to Scotland and many of the rivalries refused to be stilled. In the event the Midland influence in the 1920s proved stronger than that of its numerically larger rival the LNWR. Although the Midland Railway had many good points, its methods were never wholly accepted by ex-

8 The Stanier look on the LMS – a first generation domeless Class 5 4-6-0, No 5044, adds an extra coach to a northbound express at Bristol c.1936/7. (G.H. Soole collection–NRM)

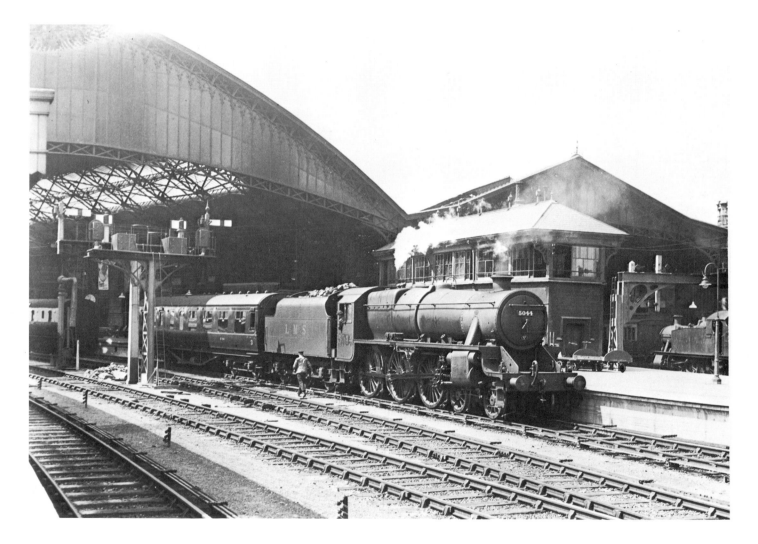

LNWR men and it seemed highly probable that when Henry Fowler (the ex-Midland CME) retired in 1930, the former Midland men would cause just as much trouble for Hewitt Beames, the next-in-line for the job and former LNWR locomotive engineer. There seemed no solution but to appoint a total outsider and this the LMS management resolved to do. Stanier was approached in 1931 and after discussing matters with Collett, his own Chief, he joined the LMS as Chief Mechanical Engineer on January 1st 1932. He was twenty years older than Gresley had been when the latter was first appointed CME. Furthermore, Stanier was given probably the most formidable task ever to be tackled by a British locomotive engineer, that of bringing order out of the chaos on what was at the time the largest joint stock corporation operating a railway anywhere in the world.

Contemporary railway observers were intrigued to see what Stanier would make of this mammoth task and there was much speculation as to the amount of 'Wiltshire Wisdom' which

would be brought to bear on the LMS system. Not surprisingly many of the solutions turned out to be pure Churchward. At the same time, Stanier was no GWR bigot and showed a constant readiness to change his ideas if events proved him wrong – as they sometimes did. In this respect he was probably less of an autocrat than Gresley and it is perhaps as well – for at the time, he possessed nothing like the reputation of his East Coast contemporary. Fortunately Stanier's work was made easier by the generally welcome reception he was given by his new colleagues, most of whom were probably heartily glad of any excuse to terminate the earlier arguments and get on with the job. Hewitt Beames probably best summed it up when he wrote a welcome letter to Stanier saying among other things 'You will understand how disappointed I am, but I may say there is no one I would rather work under than you.'

That Stanier succeeded in his brief is a matter of history and, moreover, most of his designs had emerged in the astonishingly short space of

9 Rebuilt Scots Nos 46115 *Scots Guardsman* and 46105 *Cameron Highlander*, at Carlisle in 1949 display the post- and pre-smoke deflector variations of this celebrated Stanier 4–6–0 type.
(G.L. Wilson)

five years. His policy was to be a continuation of an already partly established 'scrap and build' philosophy. One writer has called it a 'mighty re-stocking' and this is no less than the truth, for by the outbreak of World War II there were almost as many Stanier-designed engines to be seen running on the LMS as those of Gresley on the LNER, and eventually the Stanier designs achieved a considerable numerical superiority. The consequences were profound, for the LMS locomotive department under Stanier emerged from being possibly the most backward of the four British companies in 1933 to a point, some 15 years later, where it had established a reputation for building and operating steam motive power to meet modern operating conditions which was unmatched in Britain. Many members of Stanier's team were to form the essential nucleus of the design group responsible for introducing the British Railways standard locomotive classes after Nationalisation in 1948.

Stanier himself was seconded as Scientific Adviser to the Ministry of Production in 1942, was knighted in 1943 and was also elected to Fellowship of the Royal Society. He formally resigned from the LMS in 1944; but his influence lived on in his successors. In fact it was probably Stanier's major achievement that he had managed to draw together the rival factions on the LMS which had led to his appointment in the first place; and he left behind him a united and highly competent team. This was in marked contrast to the uncertainty which followed Gresley's sudden removal from the LNER picture. Furthermore, the Great Western Railway had tended since the 1920s to remain content with its earlier successes under Churchward and Collett and the Southern Railway had largely opted for electrification. It was therefore no real surprise that British Railways steam development was in many respects in direct lineal succession to Stanier's policies on the LMS railway. For one man to achieve this much via a railway which on his accession was almost a laughing stock in locomotive terms was no mean achievement.

Stanier lived on in honourable retirement as the 'Grand Old Man' of British locomotive engineers until 1965 when at the ripe age of 89

10 Class 8F 2–8–0 No 48412 was built at Swindon during the war. The non-standard ejector on the left-hand side of the smokebox was fitted to all Swindon built 8Fs to enable them to create the 25 inches of vacuum needed for working on the GWR. (T.E. Williams collection– NRM)

he died. He did not live to see the end of steam on British Railways, but it is perhaps fitting that the BR 'Farewell to Steam' special trains in 1968 were hauled by engines of his design or inspiration.

These then are the two men whose centenary was being celebrated when the first edition of this book appeared. Very different in personality and working for two railways whose respective attitudes were frequently as different as the engineers who served them, Stanier and Gresley had in common a dedication to the task of perfecting railway engineering in the environment in which they found it. 'By their fruits ye shall know them', and on this yardstick Sir Nigel Gresley and Sir William Stanier deserve to rank with the greatest of locomotive engineers of this country.

11 An impressive pre-war view of 'Princess Royal' Class 4–6–2 No 6206 *Princess Marie Louise* on Bushey troughs c.1937.

2

Gresley's work on the Great Northern

On his appointment in 1911 to succeed H.A. Ivatt as Locomotive, Carriage and Wagon Superintendent, Gresley returned to locomotive responsibilities after a gap of eleven years. It was almost a foregone conclusion that there would be innovation in Great Northern Railway locomotive development. However, before becoming immersed in his locomotives, a look at the changes which occurred in carriage and wagon design and development during the six years Gresley was in charge of that department is revealing.

The GNR had introduced the dining car, side corridor, Pullman vestibule and buck-eye coupler to Britain. In 1905, however, Gresley found large numbers of six and eight-wheeled non-bogie coaches, with vestibuled stock having wooden underframes, clerestory roofs and heating by the steam storage system.

ECJS bogie luggage van No. 126, built the following year, had an elliptical roof with bow-ends, Pullman vestibules, buck-eye couplers, steel underframe and teak body. As the prototype Gresley main-line vehicle it set the style for all subsequent passenger stock built for the GNR and LNER during the next thirty-five years. Its appearance so impressed the respective managements of the East Coast Railways that it was decided the Gresley exterior pattern should become the standard for all future Joint Stock coaches, whether built at Doncaster or York. Articulated coaches were introduced in 1907 and as well as being extensively used on the GNR and LNER the system was later to be taken up by both the GW and LMS railways and is now a feature of the French TGV. Adoption of the Spencer double-bolster carriage bogie as standard completed the impressive list of main features introduced in this period which made GNR and LNER passenger rolling stock so distinctive in appearance and so safe and comfortable to ride in.

From a number of special vehicles produced in the period, mention must be made of the Royal Saloon built in 1908 for King Edward VII. Instantly recognizable with its deep 'bowstring' frame, even though the beautiful varnished teak is now covered with claret coloured paint, this magnificent vehicle is now preserved in the National Railway Museum.

12 One of the first Gresley coaches for the GNR open third brake No 1797 built in 1906.

On the wagon side Gresley was not idle, and the 35 ton capacity vacuum-braked bogie wagons introduced in 1906 were a great advance on the 8 ton four-wheelers previously employed on the Peterborough to London brick trains. For special traffic a novel 40 ton capacity girder well wagon was designed and built for the conveyance of heavy machinery and large boilers. Always a believer in practical tests, Gresley had it run round the works yard loaded with Stirling 4–2–2 No 221.

It may seem strange in the light of future events that for the first ten years of the Gresley régime all new locomotives were intended for freight traffic. A railway CME is, however, required to meet the needs of the operating department, and in the early years of the twentieth century there was a trend throughout the country towards faster goods train services. Although the GNR was in the forefront of this movement it did not possess any locomotives really suitable for working the traffic.

13 Howldon six wheelers rebuilt by Gresley to form twin articulated set No 2710.

14 40-ton capacity girder well wagon No 46478 in Doncaster Works Yard, with Single No 221 as a test load.

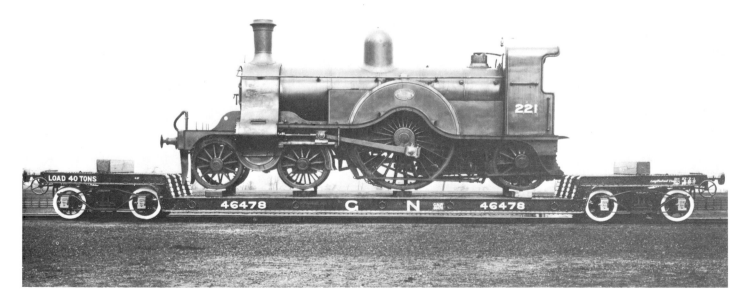

Two versions of superheated 0–6–0s with 5 ft 2 in and 5 ft 8 in diameter wheels were introduced in 1911 and 1912 for express goods work but the first Gresley design was a true mixed traffic locomotive. Although the cab, footplate fittings and tender of the new 2–6–0 were in the Great Northern tradition, the use of outside cylinders with Walschaerts valve gear, cylindrical smokebox and running plate curved gracefully over the 5 ft 8 in coupled wheels proclaimed the hands of the new master. The 20 in cylinders were supplied with steam from a 4 ft 8 in diameter boiler via 10 in piston valves, special attention being given to ensure large exhaust openings at short cut-offs. The pony truck was of a double-bolster swing link design patented by Gresley. This arrangement overcame the basic shortcoming of the ordinary swing link truck and ensured equal wheel loading under all conditions of running while still retaining the centralising control.

Ten locomotives of class H2 were built, to be followed from 1914 by a further sixty-five with larger boilers of 5 ft 6 in diameter. In LNER

15 The first Gresley locomotive, Class H2 two-cylinder 2–6–0 No 1630 built in 1912.

16 A heavy freight two-cylinder 2–8–0 of Class 01, introduced in 1913, being lifted in Doncaster Works.

days, the big boilers were fitted to the original ten and the 75 locomotives which then formed Class K2, could be found working passenger and freight trains from East Anglia to the West Highland line until withdrawal of the last 'Ragtimer' in 1962, fifty years after the introduction of the pioneer No 1630.

Before leaving the Gresley two-cylinder 2–6–0s, another point is perhaps worthy of comment. When the first Thompson design, the B1 class 4–6–0, was introduced in 1942 it was described as a general utility locomotive using the cylinders of the K2, boiler of the B17 and wheels of the V2. It would seem to be more than coincidence that what was generally considered to be the best locomotive of the Thompson era, not only combined features of earlier Gresley classes, but had cylinders from his very first design.

The next Gresley design was a large 2–8–0 for the heaviest freight workings, and the only instance where he used a 28 in piston stroke. With the largest boiler yet produced at Doncaster supplying superheated steam to 21 in diameter outside cylinders having 10 in piston valves operated by Walschaerts valve gear, the new locomotives were a great advance on the Ivatt 0–8–0s.

There was a need for more powerful shunting and local freight trip locomotives in the West Riding. The working of loose-coupled trains over severe gradients of the GN lines in the Leeds–Bradford–Wakefield 'triangle' demanded greater haulage and braking power than the Stirling and Ivatt saddle tanks provided.

Utilising boilers displaced from Ivatt 0–8–2Ts and 18 in × 26 in inside cylinders with Stephenson valve gear, the new 0–6–0Ts produced had large sloping side tanks extending from cab to smokebox front giving them quite a distinctive appearance. Thirty 'Ardsley Tanks', as they were generally known, were built between 1913 and 1919, one being the subject of a superheating experiment which did not result in any appreciable economies on the type of working the locomotives performed, and was not repeated. With a slightly larger boilered version introduced in 1922, the GNR J23 class became the standard LNER shunter and totalled 102 locomotives with the final batch built in 1939. Eventually displaced by the 350 HP diesel-electric shunter, the last seven were finally withdrawn from Departmental stock in May 1965.

At about the time the new shunters were introduced, Gresley designed his own superheater which consisted of two separate headers connected by the elements. Each element had four lengths of tube, one return loop being located in one flue tube and the other in the flue immediately below. It was claimed that an 8% gain in heating surface was attained compared with the Robinson superheater, with

17 Standard shunting and local trip working locomotive, Ardsley tank LNER Class J50, No 610.

the added advantages that all elements were interchangeable and any individual one could be changed without disturbing the others.

During the First World War Doncaster works was fully committed to the manufacture of armaments, including the provision of two armoured locomotives for coastal defence artillery trains. This preoccupation did not, however, prevent locomotive design work for the future proceeding. In 1915 a four-cylinder Pacific design was produced, which was said to have been a combination of the Ivatt large boiler Atlantic and Churchward four-cylinder locomotives. From published drawings it seemed to have more in common with GNR than Swindon practice. To test the proposed front-end, Atlantic No 279 was rebuilt with four piston valve cylinders having two sets of outside Walschaerts valve gear. A 24-element superheater was also fitted, but despite its increased tractive effort, the rebuild did not appear to make a favourable impression, although it ran in its four-cylinder form until again rebuilt in 1938.

Gresley then turned his attention to the alternative of three-cylinder propulsion which had already been applied to a number of locomotives on the NE and GC railways. Amongst advantages claimed were reduced coal consumption, less tyre wear with increased mileage between general repairs and more uniform starting effort allowing a lower permissible factor of adhesion. One of the benefits to be gained from using four cylinders

18 The Patent Gresley Superheater.

19 Experimental rebuilt version of Ivatt Atlantic No 279 with four-cylinders to try out the front end of the proposed first Pacific design.

was that only two sets of valve gear were necessary, although a number of designs still utilised four independent sets of gear. Gresley considered that the main objection to the use of three cylinders would be overcome if some practical means could be devised whereby only two sets of valve gear were necessary.

Whilst at Swindon, H. Holcroft had been granted a patent in 1909 for various alternative three-cylinder systems, but Churchward was too committed to four cylinders for any of them to be applied to GWR locomotives. Gresley's patent for two forms of conjugated valve gear was granted in 1915 and three years later one of these was put into practice.

The first three-cylinder locomotive built in Britain with only two sets of valve gear was 2–8–0 No 461, turned out of Doncaster works in May 1918. All three cylinders were inclined at 1 in 8, (the amount necessary for the middle crosshead to clear the leading coupled axle) and drove the second pair of 4 ft 8 in driving wheels with cranks set at 120°. The two outside Walschaert valve gears operated the outer arms of rocking shafts which worked the valves of the outside cylinders. Arms at the other end of each shaft were attached to the levers operating the middle valve, the two to one ratio being obtained by making one of the inner arms half the length of the others. This arrangement gave rise to

20 Britain's first three-cylinder locomotive with only two sets of valve gear. Gresley 2–8–0 No 461 built in 1918.

21 Layout of the simplified 2–1 lever form of conjugate valve gear applied to all Gresley three-cylinder piston valve locomotives built after No 461.

considerable criticism, both with regard to the extra number of pin joints compared with a third independent valve gear and the inclination of the outside cylinders. Although no further examples were built with the rocking shafts arrangement, it did work well in practice when applied to a slow-running freight locomotive and No. 461 ran unaltered for 30 years until finally withdrawn 1948.

The development of the conjugate valve gear has been the subject of considerable controversy, but Gresley certainly gave the credit to Holcroft for having first devised the arrangement whereby only two valve gears were necessary for a three cylinder locomotive. It was also Holcroft who suggested the means by which the alternative simple lever form of the Gresley patent could be applied to any three-cylinder locomotive.

The well known two to one lever form of conjugate valve gear, subsequently fitted to all Gresley three-cylinder piston valve locomotives, was first applied to a new series of mixed traffic 2–6–0 introduced in 1920. Other innovations included a 6 ft diameter boiler, twin regulator handles and the use of nickel-chrome steel for coupling and connecting rods. The 8 in piston valves had $1\frac{1}{2}$ in lap and a maximum travel of $6\frac{3}{8}$ in at 75% cut-off. Originally intended to be used mainly for express freight working, the new locomotives were soon hauling express passenger trains loading to 20 bogie vehicles at speeds up

22 The first locomotive fitted with the 2–1 lever valve gear, mixed traffic 2–6–0 No 1000 of Class H4 also carried a 6-foot diameter boiler.

23 Class N2 0–6–2T No 1608 designed for the King's Cross suburban services.

to 75 mph. Construction of the K3 class, as they became in LNER days, continued until 1937 and 193 examples were built. Some trouble was experienced with overtravel of the middle valve, particularly when coasting at high speed with the engine in full gear, and extra clearance was provided by modifying the steam chest cover. In addition, drivers were instructed to set the gear at 25% when coasting at speeds exceeding 25 mph but the over-travel problem was to have a profound and adverse effect on the design of the valve gear applied to the first Gresley Pacifics which appeared in 1922.

In the meantime, further three-cylinder 2-8-0s were ordered, generally similar to No 461 but utilising the simple form of conjugate valve gear as applied to the 2-6-0s. For the London suburban services a larger superheated development of the Ivatt 0-6-2T was produced and proved an instant success. After grouping, further examples were built without condensing apparatus for use in Scotland and eventually the N2 class totalled 107 locomotives. They remained a familiar sight at Kings Cross until 1962 when steam was finally displaced by diesel traction on the suburban services.

The last new locomotive design produced by Gresley for the GNR was a Pacific, but it bore little resemblance to the abortive 1915 version. With a 6 ft 5 in diameter 180 lb working pressure tapered boiler incorporating a wide firebox and combustion chamber, three 20 in cylinders and a tractive effort of 29,835 lb, the new locomotive was as big an advance on the Ivatt Atlantic as the latter was on the Stirling singles. In only one respect was the new design less than an absolute masterpiece–the valve gear, which, following the overtravel problems with the 2-6-0, had short lap valves with a maximum travel of only $4\frac{9}{16}$ in at 65% cut-off. As a result it was necessary to work the locomotive at comparatively late cut-offs with an adverse effect on coal consumption. Even so, the working of a 610 test train of 20 vehicles over the 105 miles from Kings Cross to Grantham in 122 mins, (only 2 minutes more than the 1950 'Flying Scotsman' schedule), showed that a locomotive capable of handling the heaviest express passenger trains had been produced.

The construction of a further ten Pacifics was authorised by the GNR, but the first of these, the famous *Flying Scotsman*, did not appear until February 1923 and was thus an LNER locomotive.

Although taking place after the 1923 grouping, the development of the Gresley GNR

24 The prototype Gresley Pacific No 1470 *Great Northern*, completed in April 1922.

Pacific into one of the finest express passenger locomotives ever built is worthy of mention at this juncture. In 1924, consideration was given to the fitting of long lap valve gear to permit earlier cut-off working, but the scheme was not proceeded with. Then the 1925 inter-change trials between the Gresley Pacific and Collett 'Castle' locomotives proved conclusively the superiority of the latter's performance, and a decision was made to revert to the use of long lap valve gears. After satisfactory results had been obtained by simply increasing the valve lap from $1\frac{1}{4}$ in to $1\frac{5}{8}$ in on one locomotive, all existing and future Pacifics were fitted with the re-designed valve-gear originally proposed in 1924. This also increased the valve travel from the original $4\frac{9}{16}$ in to $5\frac{3}{4}$ in at 65% cut-off and resulted in the average coal consumption when working 500-ton trains being reduced from 50 to 38 lb per mile. It was this marked improvement in coal consumption which made possible the introduction in 1928 of the non-stop 'Flying Scotsman' train between London and Edinburgh.

Gresley needed convincing that higher boiler pressures would not have an adverse effect on maintenance costs, but when in 1927 the often contradictory evidence had been carefully analysed, two Pacifics were fitted with 220 psi boilers having 43 element superheaters. Experience with these two locomotives led to the introduction the following year of the class A3 Super Pacific, forerunner of the streamlined A4.

During the twelve years Gresley had been CME of the GNR, 226 locomotives had been constructed to his designs covering almost the full range of operating requirements. All were still in service when, 25 years later, the LNER, into which group the GNR had been merged, also ceased to exist as a separate railway company.

25 Super Pacific No 2580 *Shotover.* Rebuilt to Class A3 in 1928 and fitted with a corridor tender for working the non-stop "Flying Scotsman".

3

Stanier's first four years

Stanier's mandate on the LMS was to introduce a new range of standard locomotives. Unlike Gresley, who in his early days could build upon the work of his illustrious predecessor, H.A. Ivatt, Stanier had nothing like such a good track record to follow when he arrived on the LMS in 1932. Furthermore, the need for new power was more urgent than on the GNR in 1911, where Gresley could and did take his time to develop his ideas. One cannot fully understand Stanier's work unless this fact is made clear. No engineer faced with a major problem likes to rush into matters, and one suspects that Stanier, like Gresley, would have welcomed the opportunity to experiment to a greater extent than in the event was possible. Fortunately Stanier was a mature engineer when he joined the LMS company, and having worked for thirty years under Churchward and Collett on the GWR, he probably felt much more certain of his ideas than had Gresley twenty years earlier. Not that Stanier rushed into things on his first day in office. He needed time to adjust to his new company, for the LMS was a very different organisation to the GWR and it is first necessary to sketch this background to the story.

On the LMS, the CME's department was, to a greater extent than in most companies, influenced by the traffic side which, following the Midland style of train control (developed first in 1907), tended to decide what it wanted, leaving it to the CME to produce the correct end product. Taken at face value, this seems reasonable enough but unfortunately, during the early 1920s, it had resulted in an attempt to translate the Midland Railway 'little-and-often' policy of frequent, lightly-loaded trains to the rest of the system where it did not always work. One effect of this was to lead to the construction of a large number of basically Midland compound 4–4–0s as the first string passenger types. These were admirable enough locomotives but not always big enough for the task, especially on the ex-LNWR lines, where unhappy memories of F.W. Webb's unsuccessful compounds lingered on. LMS operating policy also decreed much more double-heading when loads reached even moderate proportions and this was not liked either on the ex-LNWR lines, where loads up to 400 tons had, hitherto, regularly been hauled with nothing larger than a modest size two-cylinder simple expansion 4–4–0.

Fortunately for Stanier, the situation was not wholly beyond hope when he arrived on the scene. Some of the problems had already been identified and even partly solved. He took over control of some excellent locomotive works whose various design offices contained many extremely competent men. Some at least of their latent talent had already begun to bear fruit. The Horwich works of the former LYR had supervised the design of a very good mixed traffic two-cylinder 2–6–0 with valve events and cylinder proportions of which Churchward would have fully approved. The same basic engine unit was then equally successfully

26 Horwich 2–6–0 No 13007 (later 2707) leaves York c.1929–30 with a train of mostly ex-Lancashire & Yorkshire stock. This was an early member of a successful pre-Stanier design which he modified to produce his own 2–6–0 type.

translated to a series of fast-running 2–6–4 suburban tank engines built at Derby; while, in the same year, 1927, the LMS had introduced the famous Royal Scot type 4–6–0. The origin of this class was not without controversy and its history was in many ways part of the Stanier story and will be considered later. Suffice it to say at this point that the Royal Scots provided the urgently-needed big engine power for the West Coast route and when, three years later, the same successful engine unit was combined with a somewhat smaller boiler to produce the prototype LMS Patriot Class 4–6–0, a very competent intermediate size express type merged. The trouble was that many of the improvements which had occurred seemed to have arrived in spite of rather than because of the system. There was no real design integration and the fundamental unity was still lacking. Thus although in engineering terms there were many promising things on the LMS, Stanier still had to weld his new company's locomotive men into a coherent and single-minded team.

Inevitably, the first new engines to appear

27 Patriot Class 5XP 4–6–0 No 45516 *The Bedfordshire and Hertfordshire Regiment* was photographed near Byfleet with a special boat train of LNER stock on 17th February 1950. Amazingly, the locomotive still bears its pre-war red livery in remarkably good condition. This design formed the basis of the Stanier taper boiler version.

28 The first Stanier 2–6–0 No 13245 as initially turned out from Crewe Works with GWR style safety valve housing.

20

after Stanier's arrival were to designs authorised before his appointment, but it was not long before the first genuine Stanier designs appeared. Essentially, two lines of approach were adopted simultaneously; the development of existing successful designs and the introduction of totally new types. Because of the parallel work in both areas, the introduction to service of the various types, although it came rapidly, was not necessarily in the same order in which design work had been started.

The first design to be attempted was a mixed traffic 2–6–0. Further examples of this type were required and these could just as well have been a repeat of the existing Horwich design.

Stanier had no plans to perpetuate the 2–6–0 type beyond the immediate need for a few more engines of this wheel arrangement, but the need to build them must have seemed to him an ideal opportunity to try out some of his new proposals. Furthermore, it is at least possible that Stanier had also decided that one way to unity on his new company was to give a totally new look to its locomotive stock rather than perpetuate one or other of the existing standard arrangements. It is interesting, in retrospect, to realise that when Stanier's men took over design responsibility for the BR standard types they adopted much the same view. It is also interesting and yet another of those odd

29 & 30 Evolution of a Princess. The upper view shows No 6201 *Princess Elizabeth* as built with short firebox and low superheat boiler. The lower view of No 6203 *Princess Margaret Rose*, the first of the main production batch, shows the higher superheat large firebox boiler and sundry other detail changes, especially to the outside motion.

coincidences, that Stanier's first design, like that of Gresley, was a two-cylinder 2–6–0.

The Stanier 2–6–0 seems to have been designed as a sort of 'advance guard' of things to come. One eminent writer has called it a 'dress-rehearsal' for his team, and so it proved to be. All the basic Churchward design features were there; long-travel, large-sized piston valves, near horizontal cylinders, smooth internal exhaust passages, jumper-top blast pipe and, of course, a tapered domeless boiler with trapezoidal belpaire firebox. There were many smaller changes, too, in such things as big end bearings and axleboxes and when the locomotive finally emerged there was a GWR-type safety valve cover as well, put on by the drawing office to please him until Stanier had it suppressed, presumably on the basis that enough was enough! It was long thought that all official pictorial evidence of this feature had been destroyed on Stanier's orders, but some negatives have survived and one of them is reproduced here. Stanier had a marked dislike of unnecessary frills and his new 2–6–0s

were but the first examples to illustrate the neat balanced lines that were soon to become familiar on all his designs. The only reminder of the old days was the obvious Midland-pattern tender to which the engines were coupled, because Stanier's new design of tender was not worked out sufficiently early. This rather upset the visual lines of the whole ensemble, but nothing could disguise the distinctly new look which these engines represented. It was not universally liked and Herbert Chambers, the LMS chief draughtsman (an ex-Midland man), who had supervised the design of the Royal Scots, never fully accepted many of the Stanier innovations. However Chambers was moved to the post of Technical Assistant at Euston and Stanier replaced him as chief draughtsman with Tom Coleman, who had a distinctly artistic flair. It was he who gave to most Stanier locomotive classes their familiar outward details and his name deserves to be better known.

By the time the 2–6–0 design was in progress, Stanier had assembled his team and

31 No 6200 *The Princess Royal* under construction at Crew in 1933.

the main task could commence. It was conventionally expected that a new CME would design a new powerful express passenger locomotive and Stanier was no exception. The Royal Scots were handling the West Coast expresses with fair success, but train loads were still increasing and there was no great margin in reserve. A more powerful engine would clearly be needed in due course and therefore a new design made sense. However, because of the presence of the Royal Scots, the need for great numbers of new large passenger engines was not yet pressing, so Stanier decided to build but three prototype engines. In this he was expressing no more than the same engineering prudence that had marked Churchward's and Gresley's first ventures in the large passenger engine field. The design was worked out simultaneously with that of the 2–6–0 mixed traffic engines and Stanier elected to use a 4–6–2 wheel arrangement for his big passenger design. Because this was to be his first truly new departure there was an understandable desire to see it completed quickly. In consequence it actually preceded the 2–6–0 type into service

only 17 months after Stanier had arrived on the scene.

No 6200, later named *The Princess Royal*, was a truly imposing machine and by the then conventional LMS standards it must have seemed that the millennium had at last arrived. Yet this first LMS Pacific locomotive was no more than a logical development of the ideas with which Stanier was more than familiar. In many essential details it was derived directly from the GWR King class, a design with which Stanier himself had had much to do. All the important dimensions were of an identical size, even down to the last quarter inch on the cylinder diameter, and it had all the Swindon features which Stanier had decided to adopt as standard. There were some changes, however. It had four independent sets of valve gear, some LMS type detail fittings and, of course, a trailing truck and wide firebox. There may have been some thought of competing with the LNER in the choice of a 4–6–2 wheel arrangement rather than building an enlarged 4–6–0 type, but it seems much more likely that Stanier opted for the Pacific because it enabled him to use a

32 The Stanier 2–6–4T was derived from the successful Fowler version, two examples of which are shown here, Nos 2389/90, brand new in Derby paint shop. (Photomatic)

33 & 34 Domeless and domed versions of the Stanier Class 4P 2–6–4T in LMS and BR liveries respectively, Nos 2537 and 42442. The pioneer 'three cylinder' version of this type, No 2500, is preserved in the National Collection.

35 Domeless 2–6–2T No 114. This type, not the best of Stanier's designs, was, like the 2–6–4 series, developed from an earlier Fowler design. (Photomatic)

bigger boiler and firebox than was carried on the GWR 'Kings'. This arrangement provided no more theoretical power in the engine but would be useful on the long 400 mile Euston to Glasgow run. It would be particularly beneficial both on the northern gradients, where a small boiler might not possess a sufficient margin of steam to be temporarily mortgaged on the stiff banks of Shap and Beattock, and at the end of a journey where a smaller firebox might be expected to become somewhat choked up with ash and clinker.

Two engines only were built out of the planned three units, the third set of frames being kept back for a much more elaborate experimental design to be dealt with in a later chapter. Stanier's caution was well founded, for his impressive new Pacifics, like Gresley's initial 4–6–2s, were not quite correct. The engine portion gave no difficulty but the Swindon low degree superheater, coupled with the extremely long boiler (over 20 ft between tube plates), made them shy for steam. These matters were rectified in two main ways. The first two locomotives had the superheater size doubled and in the main production batch of engines

36 LMS No 145 was a later 2–6–2T with separate dome/top feed.

37 LMS No 2239 represents the wartime development of the Stanier 2–6–4T (by Fairburn) and displays the 'interrupted' front footplate. This version also had a shorter coupled wheelbase and became the basis of the BR standard 2–6–4T. (G.L. Wilson)

(Locomotives 6203–6212), introduced in 1935, this enlarged superheater was combined with slightly different boiler proportions embodying a shorter barrel and a larger firebox which contained a combustion chamber. A further improvement on one of the two pioneer engines, No 6201 *Princess Elizabeth*, was to replace the Swindon type of domeless boiler and smokebox regulator with a separate top feed and conventional dome-type regulator. This modification was later applied to all other members of the class and they became excellent engines, if not quite perhaps in the very top flight. They were very sure-footed on the banks but the four sets of valve gear and the multiplicity of lubrication points did not always endear them to the fitters and drivers.

The other totally new Stanier designs in this first phase were a two-cylinder mixed traffic 4–6–0, introduced in 1934, and a dimensionally similar 2–8–0 freight locomotive in 1935. These two were almost instantly successful straight off the drawing board and became so numerous and widespread that their story will be considered later.

Compared with the totally new designs, the Stanier standard classes, comparable with or derived from the existing LMS types, were at first something of a mixed bunch. Essentially they were taper boiler versions of the existing

2–6–4 tanks, 2–6–2 tanks and the Patriot (or 5XP) Class 4–6–0s. The 2–6–4 tank engines were highly successful machines and on some of them Stanier adopted a three-cylinder layout similar to that used in the 4–6–0s. It gave improved acceleration but showed no great saving in economy and maintenance, so the bulk of the 2–6–4Ts were built with a more conventional two-cylinder layout. A version of this design, but mounted on a more compact wheelbase chassis (to enable it to traverse rather sharper curves), was continued in production by Stanier's successor Fairburn and formed the basis of the BR standard 2–6–4 tank.

The 2–6–2 tank was developed from a Fowler design of 1930. It was a neat and compact machine which did its job well enough with no great claims to being note-worthy. Essentially it was under-boilered and had somewhat inferior valve events. A few were rebuilt with larger boilers, but the expense of converting the whole class was not really felt to be justifiable. Although hardly failures, these engines were probably Stanier's least successful achievement.

It was the Stanier version of the three-cylinder 5XP Class 4–6–0 which caused most trouble in the early days. The LMS urgently required intermediate express passenger motive power and while Stanier could afford to take

38 This view of reboilered ex-LNWR Claughton Class 4–6–0 No 5946 *Duke of Connaught* and Fowler Royal Scot 4–6–0 No 6115 *Scots Guardsman* at Crewe shows two pre-Stanier types which played their part in the Stanier story. The Claughton boiler was used on the Patriot type which led, eventually, to the Jubilees; while the Scots were, of course, transformed when rebuilt along Stanier lines.
(S.T. Cowan collection–NRM)

time developing his large express engine by building only two prototypes, no such policy was possible with the second-line express engines. In fact, such was the urgency that the parallel boiler Patriot class was built to the extent of 50 additional units during 1932–4, while Stanier's taper boiler version was being designed. Forty of these parallel boiler 4–6–0s were classed as 'Claughton rebuilds', for accountancy purposes, but all were in fact new engines.

Stanier's taper boilered version was designed for quantity production and was ordered straight off the drawing board. When first placed in service, the engines proved to be very poor steamers and there was no apparently obvious reason for this deficiency. Low degree superheat and domeless boilers tended to be blamed, along with several other Stanier features which the old guard did not like, but this was not the real problem. The new two-cylinder 4–6–0s with all but identical boilers (see Chapter 6) were an instant success. Enlarged superheaters and proper domes made an improvement, as they did when applied to other earlier Stanier engines, but the real trouble lay in the draughting.

Oddly enough, British steam locomotive engineers did not have a particularly scientific approach to the designing of an efficient blastpipe, although they had invented it way back in the pioneer days. Most attempts were

39/40 The two basic styles of Stanier Class 5XP 4–6–0 are shown here. No 5586 *Mysore* has the short firebox, domeless boiler whereas No 5590 *Travancore* has a long firebox domed boiler. Note the Fowler tenders, exchanged from Royal Scot 4–6–0s c.1935–6.

acceptable and some were quite good, but few seemed to take much notice of the work of William Adams on the London & South Western Railway in the 1890s, and it was left to the celebrated French engineer André Chapelon to develop improved draughting – with important consequences for both Gresley and Stanier, particularly the former (see Chapter 8).

British engineers tended to adopt an empirical approach and Stanier copied Churchward in his early blastpipe arrangements. This fitting involved a jumper-top which lifted up when the engine was working hard with a fierce blast. The jumper-top portion effectively increased the size of the blast orifice when lifted and this reduced the fierceness of the blast and

saved wear and tear on the boiler – particularly the firebox stays. Now this arrangement worked well enough on a two or four-cylinder Churchward type engine with four exhaust beats per revolution of the driving wheels and with plenty of steam being exhausted with each puff. What Stanier's team did not perhaps realise, nor in fairness did many others, was that with a three-cylinder engine, a smaller blast orifice was needed since each puff of the engine exhausted a smaller amount of steam.

Enginemen themselves often had a cure for poor steaming, and the generally adopted method for improving the blast of a badly steaming engine was to apply an unofficial (and often illegal) constricting device, or 'Jimmy',

41 No 5724 *Warspite*, with its proper Stanier tender, ascends Camden Bank with the 10.35 am to Liverpool on 23rd July 1946.

over the blast orifice at the sheds to reduce the effective size! There was, however, no really scientific method of testing locomotive draughting arrangements in Britain in those days and many of the better designs often achieved successful front end arrangements more by trial and error than by any more refined technique.

Thus, it took a little time to isolate the problem with the Stanier Jubilees, as the 5XPs came to be called after 1935 when the first named example was christened *Silver Jubilee*. Once effected, this change transformed the engines and they became competent and valuable machines. Although never the most widely acclaimed of Stanier's designs, the Jubilees had their moments and one of them, No 5660 *Rooke*, did some particularly fine work, for an engine of modest proportions, when put under test in 1937. Even though the parallel boiler Patriots were every bit as speedy as the later engines, Stanier's much-loved taper boiler and other features gave the Jubilees a competitive edge in terms of maintenance and other costs. It fell to the Jubilees to be the last Stanier express engines to remain in service and three of them are, happily, preserved.

Experience with the Jubilees tended to foster the impression that Stanier did not really like three-cylinder engines and it is true that apart from this class and the few 2–6–4 tanks above mentioned, he only designed two- or four-cylinder machines. However, to keep the balance straight, it should be born in mind that one of Stanier's finest achievements (some would say *the* finest) was his rebuilt version of the three-cylinder Royal Scot class and this will be considered in Chapter 7.

In the field of carriage design, Stanier is, perhaps, less well known than Gresley. In 1923, the LMS fell heir to the very fine coachbuilding traditions of both the LNW and Midland Railways, and by the time Stanier arrived on the scene, the LMS main line carriage fleet could stand comparison with the best. The coach chassis was a highly standardised and reliable unit so Stanier made few changes beyond the widespread introduction of welded construction as the years went by. However, the bodies were a little old-fashioned and Stanier quickly introduced a smooth sided, flush-clad body style derived, not surprisingly, from contemporary Swindon practice. He also incorporated other GWR features such as shell pattern roof ventilators, sliding upper window sections and suspended gangways. Together all these features soon established a distinctive Stanier 'look' to LMS expresses. Finally, and not least significantly, it was the Stanier coach which was responsible for a much more widespread

42 A typical Stanier coach – composite No 6805 – built during the mid-1930s, along with hundreds of others bearing similar outline.

43 Experimental LMS three-car diesel articulated unit. It was painted bright red and cream.

abandonment of individual compartment doors on side-corridor stock and the general provision of armrests and courtesy lights for the third class passenger.

Moving a little ahead in time, it is worth mentioning that in 1937, Stanier authorised some articulated coaches, based on the Gresley single-pivot principle, but these were not repeated. However, it is worth noting that he introduced a new double-pivot articulation joint on the 'Coronation Scot' set of vehicles built in 1939 which, sadly, never entered revenue service as such because of the war. This new articulation principle was first evaluated on an experimental three-car diesel unit which gave

evidence that Stanier, like Gresley, was not unaware of the development of other forms of traction.

By the end of 1935, Stanier could have cause for quiet satisfaction. In only four years he had introduced all but two of his standard designs, built over 500 of them and had 300 more on order. The early wranglings on the LMS were mostly a thing of the past, his engines were now working well and universally liked by the enginemen, there had only been two really worrying areas of teething trouble (the two prototype 4–6–2s and the three-cylinder 4–6–0s) and these were now behind him. All told, it was not a bad start.

4

Experimental locomotives

By the 1920s and 1930s, the conventional reciprocating steam locomotive with its fire tube boiler had achieved a high level of performance and reliability and the developments made by Churchward on the Great Western Railway during the early 1900s had begun to permeate throughout the country. Yet it was not to be expected that men of the calibre of Gresley and Stanier would remain indifferent to the claims of other, less conventional ways of converting potential energy into useful work.

When the results of the LNER/GWR interchange trials had been assimilated and the Gresley 4–6–2s with modified valve gear began to turn in the sort of performances which potentially had always been there, one senses that Gresley felt himself free to pursue some of his more experimental ideas. Some of these ideas never progressed beyond the drawing board stage but are, nevertheless, of more than passing interest.

In a paper given to the Institution of Locomotive Engineers in 1947, Bert Spencer, one of Gresley's technical assistants, gave outline details of a number of these might-have-beens and the reasons why they never became reality. Among those mentioned were a very unconventional 4–4–0 with a six-cylinder 'V' form uniflow engine and rotary cam valve gear, an articulated 2–6–4–4 development of the K3 class, a variety of two- and three-cylinder tank locomotives for both passenger and freight work and a mixed traffic 2–8–0 for the West Highland line. For express passenger work a large three-cylinder 4–6–0, more powerful than a B17, but with a greater route availability than the V2 class, was designed together with a

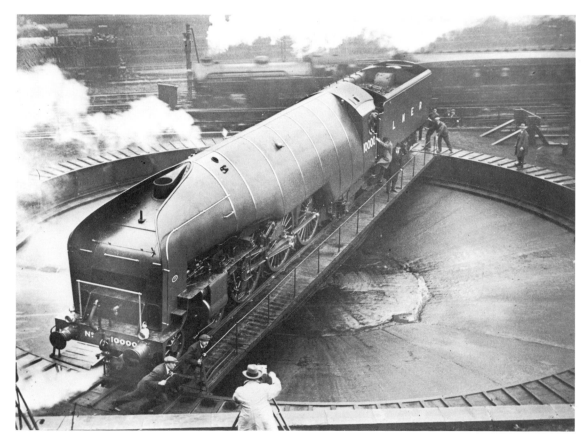

44 Water-tube boilered four-cylinder compound 4–6–2–2 locomotive No 10000, built at Darlington in 1929, on the King's Cross station turntable.

'Super A4' and a huge 4–8–2 with a tractive effort of 45,700 lb. It was said in the paper that but for the intervention of the Second World War, there was every prospect of the two latter designs being built. They would certainly have provided an interesting comparison with the proposed Stanier 4–6–4 and 4–8–4 types.

One of the tasks facing the staff of the National Railway Museum is to sort, catalogue and store in a secure but easily retrievable manner, some 100,000 engineering drawings relating to locomotives and rolling stock. Already some most interesting things have come to light, particularly amongst the Gresley era Doncaster batch. There are drawings for four variations of a scheme to alter the Class R1 0–8––2T locomotives for diesel–compressed air operation, with 400 HP 8-cylinder diesel engine coupled to a four-cylinder air compressor replacing the boiler. An undated sketch outlines

a 2–10–2 freight version of the standard Pacific which appears to pre-date the P1 class 2–8–2 built in 1925. Variations on the A4 theme include both larger firebox and higher boiler pressure versions, as well as streamlined casings for both the GN Atlantic and the V2 type.

One very unconventional locomotive which did see the light of day was the unique high-pressure four-cylinder compound No 10000, completed in 1929. The last compound locomotive design built for a British mainland railway, it had many interesting features, not least the boiler which was a water-tube marine type with a working pressure of 450 lbs per square inch. The valves of all four cylinders were operated by the two outside Walschaerts valve gears, but it was possible to vary the cut-off of the high and low pressure cylinders independently.

As was to be expected with such a novel

45 The Yarrow–Gresley water-tube boiler for No 10000 at the Yarrow Works in January 1929.

design, there were many teething troubles. Modifications to the boiler eventually allowed the locomotive to cover a daily roster of 420 miles, and for a few days it even worked the prestigious non-stop 'Flying Scotsman'. However, the hoped-for economies in fuel consumption resulting from the high boiler pressure and compound expansion never materialised. In 1935, a Kylchap double chimney was fitted and dynamometer car tests carried out between Leeds and Hull utilising the counter pressure locomotive No 761. Towards the end of the trials an average horse power of 1400 at 60 mph was maintained for nine miles, followed by an average of 1520 at the same speed for eight miles when full boiler pressure was maintained with cut-offs of 50 and 45% in high and low pressure cylinders. Despite these quite impressive results. No 10000 showed a heavier coal consumption, higher building and maintenance cost, inferior performance, availability and reliability compared with a standard Pacific; so it is not really surprising that the locomotive was rebuilt in conventional form as a three-cylinder simple in 1937. Once again, a brilliant attempt to improve on the low overall efficiency of the basic simple Stephenson type locomotive had failed to produce a winner.

After No 10000, Gresley made no further attempts at compound expansion or the use of ultra-high boiler pressures, although the original scheme for the V4 locomotive included a boiler working at 300 lbs per square inch. He was, however, convinced that independently

46 The cab of No 10000.

47 No 10000 under test with the ex-NER dynamometer car behind the tender, at Dunfermline. (R.D. Stephen collection – NRM)

48 Rebuilt in 1937 as a three-cylinder simple with conventional boiler and A4 type streamlining, No 10000 on express passenger train duty.
(Rev. A.C. Cawston collection –NRM)

49 Two ex-GCR four-cylinder 4–6–0s of LNER Class B3 were fitted with Caprotti rotary Cam Poppet valves in 1929, to be followed by two more, including No 6167, with an improved version in 1938/9.

controlled inlet and exhaust valve events were essential if a substantial improvement in cylinder performance was to be realised. Some passenger and freight locomotives of GER design had been fitted with Lenz poppet valves in the 1920s and these were followed by the rebuilding of two GCR four-cylinder 4–6–0s with Caprotti gear.

Later batches of the D49 class 4–4–0s were built with both oscillating and rotary cam valve gears but none of the applications were to high power locomotives of modern design. However, in 1934 these criteria were met with a vengeance.

50 Gresley Class D49 4–4–0 No 365 *The Morpeth* fitted with infinitely variable rotary Cam Poppet valve gear.

51 Gresley's greatest step forward Class P2 2–8–2 express passenger locomotive No 2001 *Cock o' the North* as built at Doncaster in 1934.

Cock o' the North was the apt name given to the most powerful and first eight-coupled express passenger locomotive built for service in Britain. Designed to work 550 ton trains at high average speed over the heavily graded route between Edinburgh and Aberdeen the locomotive had a number of experimental features.

Steam distribution to the three 21 in × 26 in cylinders was by Lenz rotary cam poppet valve gear. The inlet and exhaust valves were 8 in and 9 in diameter respectively, all six being operated

52 *Cock o' the North*, on trial between King's Cross and Doncaster, fitted with indicator shelter and instrumentation. (Rev. A. C. Cawston collection–NRM)

53 No 2001 on test on the Vitry Test Plant rollers in December 1934.

by two separate cam boxes, one on each side of the locomotive. In the mid-gear 'coasting' position, the exhaust valves of all three cylinders were held off their seats. Originally the steam cut-off was infinitely variable, but after a short time in service, trouble with the continuous inlet cams necessitated their replacement with the stepped type which restricted the forward gear cut-off positions to six.

Gresley's friendship with the great French locomotive engineer André Chapelon, and admiration for his work, was no secret and a number of Chapelon features were incorporated in the design. These included Kylchap double blastpipe, internal streamlining of steam passages, ACFI feed water heater and V-shaped cab front.

54 Mono block three-cylinder and smokebox saddle casting showing location of steam chests and Poppet valves.

55 Second member of the P2 class *Earl Marischal* as built with piston valves operated by Gresley–Walschaerts valve gear and additional smoke deflectors.

56 *Cock o' the North* as rebuilt in 1938 with streamlined front-end and piston valve cylinders.

Before being sent to Scotland *Cock o' the North* was tried out between Kings Cross and Doncaster on both special test and service trains. A 650 ton load was hauled up Stoke bank at an average speed of over 60 mph with the locomotive developing a drawbar horsepower of 2090. Speeds of up to 85 mph were attained with ease on the service trains. On the road for which designed, a 586 ton test train was taken from Edinburgh to Aberdeen and back, whilst in normal service 550 tons were hauled from Aberdeen to Montrose in eight minutes less than the Pacific timing for a 440 ton maximum load.

At the end of 1934 the locomotive was shipped to France for further trials, both on the road and Vitry Test Plant, but the results were not published. O.V.S. Bulleid, then Gresley's principal assistant and later CME of the SR, was in charge and twelve years later stated that the coal consumption per drawbar horsepower hour on the test plant compared favourably with the French engines, whilst on the road a horse power in the order of 2800 was developed. He maintained that the high coal consumption on the Aberdeen road was not due to the inefficiency of the locomotive, but to misuse! There was probably some truth in this, but the excessive clearance volumes and lack of infinite variation of cut-off with the stepped cam arrangement were factors not conducive to economical working.

The second member of the class was built with 9 in piston valves operated by Walschaerts–Gresley valve gear and an exhaust injector was fitted instead of the feed-water heater. *Earl Marischal* proved to be more economical in coal consumption and the four later streamlined P2s built in 1936 all had piston valves. *Cock o' the North* was fitted with piston valve cylinders and the streamlined front end in 1938. One of the

later batch was fitted with an experimental exhaust by-pass arrangement to reduce the tendency of the blast to lift the fire when starting or working at long cut-offs, but a refinement of the idea developed early in 1941 was never carried out.

There were insufficient passenger trains loaded to over 500 tons on the Aberdeen route to utilise fully the six locomotives, with the result that many workings were 'over-engined'. The eight-coupled axleboxes did not take kindly to the numerous curves on the route, and with Pacific train loads the P2s were expensive to both operate and maintain.

It is a great pity that their prodigious haulage capacity could not have been used to assist in the working of the enormous wartime loads between Kings Cross and Newcastle. Certainly there would have been ample opportunity for them to be run under near optimum operating, if not maintenance, conditions in relation to power output and adhesion. However, it was not to be. There was no place for Gresley 'super-power' in the strategy of the new CME and all the P2 class locomotives were rebuilt by Thompson into ungainly Pacifics. As 4–6–2s, they had a very short life on the Aberdeen road and had all been scrapped before the end of 1961.

Whatever the merits or shortcomings of *Cock o' the North*, it probably represented Gresley's greatest single step forward and was certainly ahead of its time. It is significant that when, twenty years later, the last express passenger steam locomotive was built for British Railways, it had three cylinders fitted with poppet valves.

While Gresley was pursuing his various experiments on the LNER, Stanier was settling in to his new LMS appointment and experimental work was hardly part of his brief in those first years. Furthermore, he was still 'on

57 Stanier's experimental turbine 4–6–2 No 6202 as built with medium superheat domeless boiler. This side of the boiler carried the forward turbine.

probation' as it were and, as has been recorded, not all his new engines were an instant success. Fortunately, Stanier was a big enough man to make the necessary changes and by 1935, when matters looked set fair for him, his one notable experimental locomotive appeared, the turbine-driven 4–6–2 No 6202.

Stanier was not really an inventor. Unlike Gresley, no patents stand to his name and his real strength lay in a knowledge of current techniques and an ability to put them into practice to give the best return, taking all factors into account. This is a far less glamorous approach, but in cost-effective terms probably more useful to railway management. In particular, Stanier paid constant attention to running and maintenance costs and it is probably for this reason that he became attracted to the idea of turbine drive. In 1932, his attention had been drawn by Dr H. L.Guy, of Metropolitan-Vickers, to a very interesting experiment in Sweden with a non-condensing

turbine-driven 2–8–0 which, on test, seemed to promise coal and water savings of between 7% and 15% compared with reciprocating locomotives. But Stanier also foresaw a potential maintenance saving, partly because of the simplicity of the moving parts resulting from the elimination of conventional cylinders and valve gear, but also because of the more efficient lubrication of the totally enclosed drive mechanism. Accordingly, one set of frames built for the three planned prototype 4–6–2s was set aside in 1933 for use on an experimental turbine engine in collaboration with Dr Guy and Metropolitan-Vickers.

The year 1934 was fully occupied with sorting out the teething troubles of the two new Pacifics and the troublesome Class 5XP 4–6–0s, but by mid-1935, the experimental work could start. No 6202 emerged in June, a few weeks before the main production batch of ten additional Princess type Pacifics with which it shared many features in common, notably a much improved boiler. On

58 'Turbomotive' as running later with high superheat, domed boiler. This side carried the reverse turbine.

emerging from works it was seen to be a very handsome variation of the Princess Royal type.

Several theoretical advantages accrue from the use of turbine propulsion. The turbine itself imparts, via the drive unit, a continuous rotary motion to the road wheels. This not only eliminates the 'hammer blow' associated with reciprocating parts, but also produces a continuous exhaust at the blastpipe. This has two beneficial effects. The absence of hammer blow permits an increased static axle loading (with consequentially enhanced adhesion weight) and the continuous exhaust is not only less fierce than with a conventional engine, but also puts far less mechanical strain on the boiler and firebox than does the rhythmic suction effect of conventional exhaust beats. To compensate for the different draughting characteristics, No 6202 was always fitted with a double chimney and, shortly after being built, the boiler was altered to give a larger free gas area through the tubes than on the standard Princess type.

It is no exaggeration to say that for an experimental machine, *Turbomotive*, as it was always nicknamed, was a considerable success. Always a popular engine with the footplate crews, even if a bit 'dirty' to operate, No 6202 proved capable of handling any task set to the conventional 4–6–2s. On test it could indicate over 2300 horse power at over 70 miles per hour with a near 500 ton load on a gradient of 1 in 300; and at an evaporation rate of 20,000 lbs of steam per hour it could put out some 12% more horse power than a conventional Princess type with no significant increase in coal consumption.

Offsetting these very real improvements in performance were a lower average annual mileage than the Princess type (although still a very creditable 54,000 miles per year until the outbreak of war), a much higher first cost, higher maintenance costs and more time out of service awaiting spare parts. These factors mostly stemmed from the 'one-off' nature of the project, and a whole class of such machines would probably have proved capable of competing more effectively with conventional types – but this was never to happen. First, the war intervened and the cost of maintaining a single experimental locomotive rapidly became prohibitive, especially if the engine lay out of service for long periods awaiting spare parts. These, of course, could not be given any sort of priority in those days. The second reason for the abandonment was almost certainly the success of Stanier's later design of conventional 4–6–2, the Coronation Class, which, in terms of power output, measured scientifically, out-performed not only all its LMS rivals but those of the other British companies too.

No 6202 survived the war and ran as a turbine engine until 1950 when the cost of replacing the turbines was considered too high and the engine was rebuilt conventionally as a modified Princess Royal type but with a front end arrangement based on the Coronation

59 A rare view of 6202 running tender first, southbound at Bushey, on empty stock.

Class. Named *Princess Anne*, it ran but 11,000 miles in this form before being wrecked beyond economical repair in the frightful Harrow double collision of 1952.

So it was that the most noteworthy experimental projects of both Gresley and Stanier came largely to nought, although it would be wrong to call them in any sense failures, since much useful data was gained.

Perhaps the most useful lesson learned, in terms of subsequent history at all events, was that the conventional reciprocating locomotive, taking all things into consideration, was still the most reliable and practicable means of harnessing steam power to railway use; apart, that is, from direct electric traction which, of course, has its steam engines in the power station.

60 Eventually, the turbine locomotive ran with smoke deflectors and came thus to BR when it was renumbered 46202 and painted in lined black, the former LNWR livery.

61 'Turbomotive' rebuilt as a conventional four-cylinder reciprocating type, No 46202 *Princess Anne*.

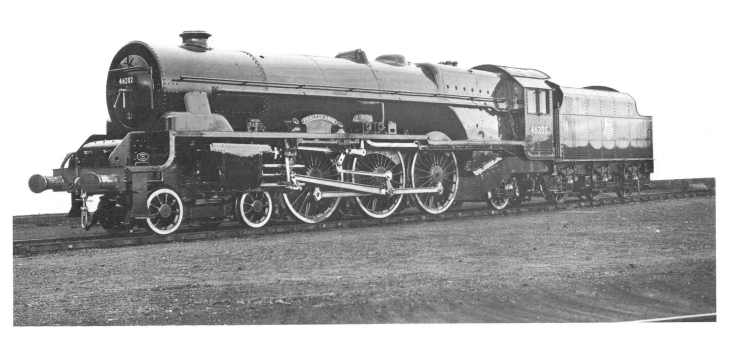

5

Freight power

On most British railways, although the long distance express might be more in the public eye, it was freight which provided the major part of the operating revenue. So we now turn to the contribution made by Gresley and Stanier to the business of moving the nation's goods traffic. As in many matters concerning these two men, the respective railway environments in which they worked were probably to prove the major influence.

The foundations for LNER freight locomotives had been well and truly laid in pre-grouping days and with one solitary exception, all new additions to stock exclusively for this class of work were to constituent company

designs or developments thereof. As was to be expected the Gresley three-cylinder 2-8-0 became, as class O2, the standard heavy freight locomotive and continued in spasmodic production until 1943. They were, however, always greatly outnumbered by the Robinson ROD type two-cylinder 2-8-0s which as class O4 totalled 421 locomotives in LNER stock with the 273 bought from the Government. The GCR also provided 89 class Q4 0-8-0s and 274 J11 0-6-0s, all three types which, in modified form, were to cover future freight requirements under Thompson's 1945 standardisation programme.

In addition to the Gresley designs, the GNR provided 55 Ivatt 0-8-0s and various 0-6-0 types including 110 piston valve superheated examples dating from 1911.

From the NER came three types of 0-8-0, the largest numerically being the 120 locomotives of class Q6 which were to continue as the mainstay of heavy freight workings in the North East until the end of steam there in 1967. The most modern in design were the massive three-cylinder Q7s, with a tractive effort of 39,963 lb. Introduced in 1919, a further ten were built in 1924. Of 0-6-0s the most numerous were the class J27 which were to total 115 on completion of the last ten superheated examples in 1923.

The GER contribution included four classes of sound 0-6-0, the largest of which were the most powerful of this wheel arrangement in the country. Finally from the NBR came three versions of 5 ft wheel diameter 0-6-0, some

62 The LNER standard heavy freight locomotive, Gresley Class 02 2-8-0 No 3834. Built in 1942, this example is coupled to a GCR tender made available by the rebuilding of a Class Q4 0-8-0 to Q1 0-8-0T.

examples of which survived until the end of steam in Scotland and unusually for the type, bore names.

Despite being well served by inherited freight locomotives, the first four new LNER designs were all of this type, and it was not until 1927 that a new passenger example appeared.

Regarded by O.V.S. Bulleid as the best looking engine Gresley ever built, the two 2-8-2 Pl class mineral locomotives turned out of Doncaster works in 1925 were designed to work 1600 ton trains of 100 wagons between Peterborough and London. As a freight development of the Gresley Pacific, they shared the same boiler, cylinders and valve gear, but had 5 ft 2 in diameter driving wheels and a six-wheeled tender. To assist in starting heavy loads, a 'booster' engine was fitted on the trailing carrying wheels.

In service, the great length of trains the P1s were able to handle proved something of an embarrassment to the Operating Department and the boosters were found to be unnecessary and removed. In 1934 No 2394 was tried on passenger train working between Kings Cross and Peterborough and easily maintained a speed of 65 mph. When the 180 lb boilers were due for renewal they were replaced by the 220 lb version and the cylinder diameter reduced to 19 in as on the A3 class. With a tractive effort now of 42,460 lb it was not operationally possible to utilise the two locomotives to full advantage and

63 Kitson built ex-ROD Robinson 2-8-0 purchased by the LNER and rebuilt by Gresley in 1929 with a standard Class 02 boiler.

64 Heavy freight version of the Gresley Pacific. Booster fitted Class P1 2-8-2 No 2393 at Doncaster Works in 1925.

they were withdrawn in 1945 to provide boilers for two further conversions from A1 to A3 Pacific.

The most powerful steam locomotive built for a British railway and the only LNER Garratt type No 2395 was also introduced in 1925. Built by Beyer-Peacock with a 2–8–0 + 0–8–2 wheel arrangement and 72,940 lb tractive effort, the two 'engines' were virtually interchangeable with the O2 class locomotives.

Until the line was electrified on the 1500 Volt DC overhead system, the Garratt was exclusively used banking freight trains up the three miles of 1 in 40 gradient on the Worsborough branch. After conversion to oil firing it was used for a time on the famous Lickey incline of the former Midland Railway,

being finally withdrawn at the end of 1955.

In 1926, what was to be numerically the largest class of Gresley locomotive was introduced, and a two-cylinder type at that! There were two versions of the new 0–6–0, the J38 class with 4 ft 8 in coupled wheels and J39 with 5 ft 2 in wheels. The drawings were prepared at Darlington and perhaps not surprisingly, many of the better NER features were incorporated in what was generally a development of the P3 (J27) class. With 20 in ×26 in inside cylinders, 8 in piston valves with $1\frac{1}{2}$ in lap operated by Stephenson valve gear and a free steaming boiler pressed to 180 psi the large wheeled version was frequently used on secondary passenger work. With tractive efforts of 28,414 and 25,664 lb both types were really

65 Britain's most powerful steam locomotive – the Gresley–Garratt under construction at the Beyer–Peacock Works, Gorton in 1925. The Gresley patent double bolster pony truck is at the rear of the locomotive.

66 Class U1 2–8–0+0–8–2. 87′ 3″ over buffers, and weighing 178 tons, No 2395 had a tractive effort of 72,940 lbs.

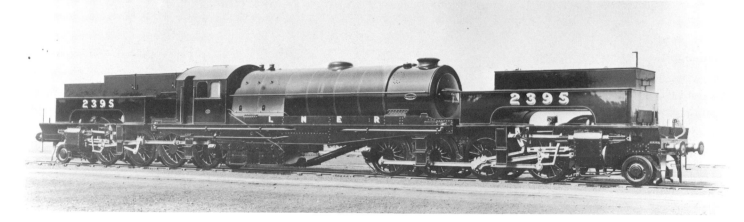

too powerful for an inside cylindered 0–6–0 if maintenance attention was to be minimised. Gresley evidently wanted to build a smaller cylindered 5 ft 2 in wheel diameter version of the K3 2–6–0 which had been designed in 1924, but financial considerations prevented the CME from getting his own way on this occasion. Eventually a very similar design of 2–6–0, the K4 class, was authorised for the West Highland line but only six were built.

Thirty five J38s and 17 J39s were built in 1926, further examples of the latter class being constructed in each subsequent year up to 1939. After a break of two years, a final batch of 18 built in 1941 brought the total number of J39s up to 289.

The J38 locomotives were used almost exclusively on freight work in Scotland, but the much more numerous J39 class saw service in most areas of the LNER, often on excursion trains and occasionally even on express passenger workings. A number of experiments

67 & 68 Variations on the 0–6–0 theme. Class J38 No 1423 has 4′ 8″ diameter driving wheels and steam reverser. The J39 No 1453 with 5′ 2″ wheels has screw reversing gear. (R.D. Stephen collection–NRM)

were tried including the fitting of Maddison crossheads and split type axleboxes to reduce maintenance costs whilst the possibility of reducing the loading on the driving anxleboxes by placing the coupling rods on the same centres as the adjacent big end cranks was also considered. To sum up, the Gresley 0–6–0s were powerful free-steaming, free-running locomotives but with the inherent weaknesses of the most typical of British wheel and cylinder arrangement.

The LNER was indeed fortunate to inherit from the constituent companies freight locomotives of generally sound design which, with relatively few additions, were able to meet freight traffic demands until finally displaced by diesel and electric traction. The 1925 dynamometer car trials between the basically similar GNR two- and three-cylinder 2–8–0s had shown the latter to have a marked economy in coal and water consumption. Gresley would no doubt have liked to build many more of them but, in the event, although the last examples were constructed as late as 1943, the class only totalled 67 locomotives including the unique No 461.

Of all the 'big-four' railways, the East Coast group suffered most from the years of industrial depression and was never in a financial position during Gresley's term of office to undertake a major locomotive re-stocking such as occurred on the LMS. The ready availability of large numbers of second-hand (and presumably cheap) ROD locomotives, identical to a numerous and efficient existing LNER type, was sure to be a more attractive proposition than new construction in the prevailing circumstances. From an accountancy point of view, it was also cheaper to put older locomotives in store during periods of traffic depression.

As a final comment on Gresley freight locomotives and particularly the P1 class, it is worth recalling that the concept of a freight version of a Pacific was again repeated with the BR standard designs. Although the 9F 2–10–0 was the type actually built, it was a 2–8–2 which was first designed to meet the heaviest freight demands of the nationalised railway system.

If Gresley's goods engines could be characterised by their variety, culminating in the highly effective 2–8–0s, this was no more than reflective of the nature of Gresley's railway and the relatively long period over which his engines were evolved and built. Stanier's single major contribution was equally a manifestation of the

69 Class K4 2–6–0 No 3441 *Loch Long*, first of six small-wheeled versions of the K3 Class built for the West Highland line and very similar to the 1924 design Gresley preferred to the inside cylinder 0–6–0. (Rev. A.C. Cawston collection–NRM)

conditions which he had to meet. It is also characteristic that his one purely freight design turned out in the end to be the most numerous single class of locomotives built for his, or any other British railway during the twentieth century.

Steam freight locomotives were normally much longer lived than contemporary passenger types and built in larger numbers. Consequently, when Stanier arrived on the LMS, he found thousands of freight engines in service,

performing their essential task tolerably well. They were not the most efficient goods engines he could have wished for, but many of them were relatively young and the need for replacement was less pressing. In particular, there were well over 700 examples of the medium sized Fowler Class 4F 0–6–0 in service. These engines were purely Midland in design, but although many had entered service prior to the grouping, most of them were built by the LMS during the mid 1920s, and had many more

70 The first few Stanier 2–8–0s were classified 7F and steam braked only. No 8003 was photographed thus at Derby c.1935/6.

71 The standard 8F is exemplified by No 8703, vacuum fitted and with a domed boiler.

years of life left in them. They were not a particularly memorable design, suffering from poor axleboxes and, at times, a shyness for steam; but their sheer numbers, rugged simplicity and ease of maintenance made them, overall, a reasonably sound investment.

The Class 4Fs were supplemented by hundreds of other older pre-group 0-6-0s, many of them excellent designs and giving varying degrees of power and efficiency. All told, they catered more than adequately for the middle and lower end of the freight power requirements of the LMS. Stanier thus had no real need to design a medium powered freight engine–nor did he do so. He undoubtedly foresaw an ultimate need for a replacement in the Class 4 power group, but it was left to one of his successors, H.G. Ivatt, actually to design such a locomotive, the rather austere 2-6-0 which was introduced in late 1947. The many different design studies made by the LMS during the years before the Ivatt design, are indicative of the less pressing need for a lower powered freight engine and it is significant that Stanier himself authorised further small batches of the standard Fowler Class 4F between 1937 and 1941. This was presumably more economical than introducing a new type of locomotive before the design had been adequately settled and when the need was for only a few engines.

The heavy freight situation on the LMS presented more of a problem to Stanier than did the lower power groups, although still not in such a pressing form as with other traffic categories. The bulk of heavy freight was handled by a large number of two-cylinder simple expansion 0-8-0s. The majority of these were of LNWR origin but a large number had come from the LYR and Fowler himself had built a sizeable batch of Class 7F 0-8-0s as a potential LMS standard in the 1920s. These latter engines were something of a near miss and they married a developed version of LNWR boiler to a basically Midland type chassis. They had a good front end but suffered even more than the 4Fs from overheating of the too small Midland type axleboxes. What with this and the fact that many of both the LNWR and the LYR types were becoming life expired, Stanier could see the need for a eight-coupled freight replacement and therefore incorporated one, a 2-8-0 type, in his proposed standard range of engines.

Stanier chose the 2-8-0 configuration rather than the 0-8-0, for a variety of reasons. He was naturally influenced by the highly successful Churchward 2-8-0s of the GWR, but regardless of this fact, the 2-8-0 arrangement gave better riding characteristics for general use and caused less wear and tear to the track than did an 0-8-0 engine. Furthermore, the Robinson 2-8-0s of Great Central design, not to mention the Gresley 2-8-0s on the East Coast route, both tended to confirm the virtues of the 2-8-0 arrangement.

When Stanier's class 7F 2-8-0s (later re-classified 8F) emerged in 1935, they showed no real surprises. A shortened version of the boiler used on his mixed traffic 4-6-0 (See Chapter 6) was fitted to a chassis with cylinders and valves of identical characteristics to those of the mixed traffic 4-6-0s. A highly successful and free-running engine was the result. As with all of Stanier's earlier designs, a low superheat boiler was first employed, but this was less of a hindrance to the 2-8-0 than to the 4-6-0s. Nevertheless, in the interests of standardisation, the bulk of the 2-8-0s were given the modified boilers with larger fireboxes and superheaters–exactly the same in fact as on many of the later series of mixed traffic 4-6-0s.

The Stanier Class 8F did not at first go into the same quantity production as had his 4-6-0 designs. This, of course, reflected the less pressing need for the engines. Even so, by 1939, 126 were in service which, by any other than Stanier standards, would have been considered reasonably rapid progress. However the Second World War was to change the picture rapidly.

As was the case during the 1914-1918

72 Darlington-built 8F for LMS service No 8500.

73 Southern-built 8F for LNER service as Class 06 No 7675.

conflict, the need was foreseen for additional locomotives both for home and overseas service; and experience a generation earlier had shown the general all-round usefulness of a 2–8–0 for such purposes. Reasons of standardisation decreed that only one design should be authorised. The Robinson 2–8–0 type (built under similar circumstances during World War I) was by now a little old-fashioned, the GWR type had restricted route availability and the Gresley 02 had conjugated valve gear – a potential maintenance problem in wartime. The choice therefore fell on the Stanier type and many hundreds more were built between 1941 and 1945 to the order of both the wartime Railway Executive Committee (for general service in Britain) and the Ministry of Supply (for the War Department overseas).

These wartime 8Fs were built by all the four British companies and by outside contractors. Many were allocated to the LMS fleet, many more to the WD and a sizeable number to the LNER, where they were classified O6. Furthermore, some of those built for the LMS were subsequently requisitioned by the WD. These widespread activities gave rise to a number of rather curious occurrences. On the one hand the Southern Railway was building engines to LMS design for the LNER while the latter company was building identical machines, lettered LMS but on loan to itself! Meanwhile at Swindon they were building engines designed by Stanier which were given LMS insignia but were on loan to the GWR for a period. History does not tell us the reaction of Stanier to all these activities, but he was probably quietly satisfied. At a later date, Swindon actually used the 8F flanging blocks for the boilers of the GWR County class 4–6–0s. Unfortunately, Swindon rather changed the internal characteristics of Stanier's boiler in this design, and the Counties were never the best of engines although by no means failures.

Eventually, 852 Class 8Fs were constructed

74 A string of 8Fs built for wartime service. The fourth engine in the row is a Westinghouse fitted WD example.

75 Detail view of Westinghouse fitted 8F No 387 for WD service.

49

but a number of these were lost at sea and others remained abroad in the service of overseas railways. At the end of the war the LNER batch was renumbered into the LMS series and lettered LMS, although some of them were only on loan from the LNER. All told, only 719 out of 852 actually ran with LMS numbers at some time or another and a few of the foreign wanderers did not return to BR service until 1957.

The Stanier 8F was also the basis for a wartime utility 2–8–0 designed by R.A. Riddles (one of Stanier's team) at a later date. The WD type, as it became known, bore little visible resemblance to a Stanier engine and the design was literally pruned down to the barest essentials to save both construction time and costs at a critical period; but it gave widespread and valuable service. During the 1940s and 1950s, many hundreds of these engines too were also to be seen at work in Britain.

Between them the 8Fs and WDs increasingly bore the brunt of much of the heavy freight working during the latter days of steam in many parts of Britain. Although eventually joined by the superb BR Class 9F 2–10–0, also conceived by Riddles, the 8Fs were never outnumbered by later designs, and right to the end they were performing the job for which they had been designed–a fate which was not always the case with some of their more exalted contemporaries.

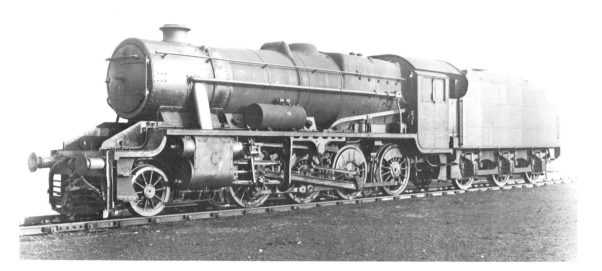

76 This view shows LMS No 8094, later WD606, at Eastleigh in 1941 having received sundry modifications for use in hot climates and poor terrain. Note the double roof cab and the "cowcatcher".

77 A typical 8F turn towards the end of steam– No 48669 at the head of a heavy train of tank wagons. (T.E. Williams collection– NRM)

6

The engines that won the war

Over the years, a tradition had become established among the railways of Britain that specific tasks needed specific locomotive types to perform them most effectively and this tradition died hard. Even when Churchward had introduced but a limited range of locomotives to handle most of the varied work on the GWR, many other lines continued to proliferate a whole variety of types from high speed express locomotives down to tiny freight engines. In themselves, many of these designs were quite good and some of them very good indeed, but the sheer variety of types involved was not conducive to a high degree of standardisation of parts nor to the reduction of maintenance costs. This was perhaps not so critical on many of the smaller companies which existed prior to 1923, but it presented the larger grouped companies, especially the LNER and LMS, with a vast variety of motive power at the time of the railway grouping.

Financial considerations were to decree that Gresley was never really allowed to solve this problem. Throughout his LNER career the company continued to exhibit an astonishing variety of locomotive types. However, the LMS had an even bigger problem than the LNER. It acquired over 10,000 locomotives of almost 400 different types in 1923, something like 30% more on each count than the LNER. This was the real problem which Stanier had to solve. The LMS had already resolved to 'scrap and build' before he arrived, and had made a tentative start, but the fundamental problem was what to build. In this situation, Stanier's GWR experience was to prove decisive.

Churchward's work on the GWR had, by the time of his retirement, produced considerable economies as a result of the widespread introduction of standard parts and practices. Common boilers for several different types of locomotive, standardised cylinder dimensions and numerous other common features, particularly in the realm of component fittings, were the norm for Swindon designs and this work was continued by Collett, assisted by

78 The first Class 5 4-6-0s to enter service had short fireboxes and domeless boiler exemplified here by No 5041 at Bow in 1938. Note the crosshead vacuum pump, later removed. (C. Cokell).

Stanier. Their particular contribution was to take the well tried Swindon No 1 boiler and the classic two-cylinder GWR 'Saint' Class 4–6–0 front end but fit 6 ft diameter wheels in place of the larger 6 ft 8 in wheels carried by the Saints. The prototype was built in 1924 (it was in fact converted from No 2925 *Saint Martin*), but it was to be the first of the famous GWR 'Hall' class 4–6–0s and the progenitor of most subsequent general purpose 4–6–0s designed in Britain.

What Collett had done was really quite simple. He had produced a truly all purpose machine which, while it could travel virtually as fast as the larger wheeled express types, could also, by virtue of its smaller wheels, handle a multiplicity of other jobs from stopping passenger services to fitted freight. Only at the extreme ends of the operating spectrum was something more specialised needed, and even here the Halls could–and did–prove a not unacceptable substitute on many occasions. The Hall class gave the lie to the perceived need for a large variety of engine classes and Stanier took this knowledge with him to the LMS where the need was far greater than on the GWR and, because of the sheer size of the LMS system, large numbers of general utility engines could be gainfully employed. Thus was born the

celebrated Stanier Class 5 4–6–0, one of the great locomotive designs of this or any other country.

So much has been written about these engines that we shall confine ourselves to but a few of the more significant facts. The engines were a truly new design as far as the LMS was concerned. The boiler was of the classic Swindon type and the two-cylinder layout exhibited the long travel, long lap valves and the adequate valve/cylinder proportions which were so much part of the GWR scene. Many of the detail fittings were of LMS inspiration, but wherever Stanier was unconvinced of the merits of traditional design, he introduced his own standards. In particular he gave the engines adequate axleboxes and, in doing so, all but eliminated the problem of overheated bearings. He also improved the valve settings over the GWR Hall which had negative lead in full gear. This made the Class 5 a rather faster engine than the Hall and the achievement of 90 mph or more was no real problem.

Where Stanier made mistakes, he generally corrected them quickly. The frames of the first examples were not as robust as traditional LMS designs and had to be strengthened, and there was, of course, the famous matter of the boilers.

79 Class 5 No 5167 displays the more common shorter chimney and top feed pipes concealed beneath the boiler cladding. Note the tablet catcher on the cabside for working on single lines in Scotland. The picture shows one such working–the 2.35 pm Perth to Inverness freight.

As with all his early designs, Stanier employed domeless boilers with a minimum degree of superheat and smokebox type regulators. These features have often been criticised in retrospect because subsequent events showed that an enlarged superheater was preferable and that a dome-type regulator gave less problems. But to get the record straight (and for other early Stanier designs, too) this had little to do with the different coal which the LMS used compared with the GWR.

Much has been published about Churchward locomotives being designed to burn South Wales steam coal and it has been suggested that boilers designed for this fuel would not perform adequately with the different types of coal found on other systems. This argument has been advanced as a reason why Stanier's early engines for the LMS did not steam too well. However, such comments seem to overlook conveniently the fact that GWR locomotives were frequently fuelled with non-Welsh coal, especially in the Midlands and around Chester and performed perfectly well. Furthermore, the GWR/LNER locomotive exchange of 1925 showed conclusively a GWR superiority even on LNER metals using hard Yorkshire coal. Stanier, therefore, had no objective evidence to suppose that GWR type boiler proportions would not work equally well on the LMS – all available evidence seemed to indicate that the classic Churchward proportions were about right.

80 Close-up of No 5429 undergoing spray painting, before the war – a somewhat unusual process for steam locomotive finishing.

81 No 45000 was not, paradoxically, the first Class 5 to appear but is the officially preserved example in the National Collection. It remained domeless right through the BR period and is still in working order, now running as LMS 5000. (M. Welch)

What had been overlooked was the question of firing. Along with the gradual development of his designs, Churchward had simultaneously encouraged a more scientific approach to locomotive firing by his footplate crews. In consequence, GWR firemen were particularly well trained in the correct techniques for firing a Churchward type engine. On the LMS, the many different pre-group companies and the many different types of engines involved had produced no such common approach. The low superheat Stanier engines needed the firing skill of GWR enginemen and at first they did not get it. Fortunately for the Class 5, however, it did not share the draughting problems of the first three-cylinder Stanier 4–6–0s (see pp 22–24), so even the low superheat engines steamed reasonably well even when fired in rather haphazard manner and as the men became more accustomed to them, they gave little trouble. In fact, quite a number retained low superheat, domeless boilers until withdrawal in the 1960s, including No 5000, preserved in the National Collection.

Perhaps the most important factor concerning the Class 5s was their universal acceptance on all parts of the system. Everywhere they went they were liked by the enginemen. With a larger superheater they responded to all manner of different driving techniques, save perhaps for ultra short cut-off working; while their clean visual lines (schemed as with most Stanier designs by Tom Coleman) suggested businesslike and capable performance. The aesthetics of the taper boiler did not please

all the die-hards and it is arguable that this type of boiler was not absolutely necessary in thermodynamic terms either on engines of medium size; but Stanier was convinced of its value and having produced an 'engineman's engine', few were inclined to quibble about such minutiae. More than any other of his designs, Class 5 finally stilled most of the conflicts which had bedevilled the LMS in its early days.

Allied to the acceptance by the footplate crews was a noteworthy maintenance record. The mileage between general repairs was good and in the final batches, averaged between 150,000 and 160,000 with, normally, an intermediate repair at about the half-way point. For a common user machine this was an enviable record. Thermodynamically the Class 5 could hold its own with any comparable design and had a good record in both economy and reliability. Over the years, many detailed refinements were incorporated to improve the locomotives still further, and by the time construction ceased, shortly after nationalisation, 842 had been built. Many of the salient features of the final versions were passed on to the BR standard Class 5 4–6–0. If one adds to this the fact that, as already related, the even larger number of Class 8F 2–8–0s took their boiler, cylinder and valve gear characteristics from the Class 5, Stanier's memorable design surely has its place in locomotive history. Stanier rarely spoke of his own engines but he seems to have liked the Class 5s: 'You see them all over the place and the drivers like them because they are such a deuce of a good engine'.

82 An example of possibly the most common Class 5 variant, No 44878, pilots a double-headed southbound express over Smardale viaduct in June 1952. (E.D. Bruton collection – NRM)

It was of course hard to ignore the work of such a large stock of almost identical locomotives all performing prodigies of work in a way which demanded universal attention. In LMS days they were far more numerous than the Class 8Fs (which did not become widespread until after 1945) and were probably the best investment the company made. Small wonder that they called them 'The engines that won the war'.

This accolade was not of course confined to the LMS Class 5. There was no doubt in LNER circles which locomotive they considered having won the war—the Green Arrow, Gresley's V2 class 2-6-2. This was a quite different locomotive to the Stanier 4-6-0 and it is the Thompson B1 which is generally considered to be the LNER equivalent of the Class 5. Of similar size and performance to its LMS predecessor, the B1 was not however put into quantity production until after the war. Although when introduced in 1942 it was said to be a combination of features from earlier Gresley locomotives, the result was very much a Thompson product and it therefore falls outside the scope of this discussion.

83 Many post-war built Class 5s had the top feed moved well forward. No 44661 displays this configuration in the late 1950s/early 1960s. (Eric Knight)

84 Among several experimental Class 5s built after the war was a particularly ugly batch of Caprotti valve gear locomotives, represented here by No 4748 in works grey finish.

The Gresley general purpose locomotive was quite different from both the Stanier and Thompson versions and owed little to Swindon. Designed in 1939, but with production first delayed by the war and then cancelled following Gresley's death after only two had been built, the V4 class 2–6–2 came too late to play a major part in moving wartime traffic. Really a big engine in miniature, the last new Gresley design to be built incorporated the outstanding features of his successful express and mixed traffic locomotives. The first example, No 3401 *Bantam Cock*, was completed at Doncaster Works in February 1941, to be followed a month later by the un-named No 3402 which differed in having an all-steel welded firebox with a single

Nicholson thermic syphon. Otherwise both locomotives shared the same features including a taper boiler with round top wide firebox, three cylinders, conjugate valve gear, 5 ft 8 in driving wheels and a tractive effort of 27,420 lb. An exceptionally high route availability of 80% of the LNER system was achieved by the extensive use of fabricated components in place of castings and nickel-steel for the boiler-barrel, coupling and connection rods. Although the V4 turned out to be an excellent performer in traffic, Gresley's successor had different ideas for a medium-sized mixed traffic locomotive and the only two examples were withdrawn in 1957 having spent most of their relatively short life working in Scotland.

85 Gresley high route availability general purpose Class V4 2–6–2 No 3401 *Bantam Cock*. Only two examples were built, the second having a steel firebox with thermic syphon.

86 The Pioneer V2 *Green Arrow* as originally turned out with curved nameplate and numbered 637.

Returning to the LNER 'War Winner', the V2 class was designed for heavy long distance work, particularly express goods and passenger trains. As a modern successor to the K3 class dating back to 1920, consideration was first given to an articulated version of the 2–6–0 with larger driving wheels and also to a three-cylinder 4–6–0, but neither of the alternative designs were built.

The first of an order for five locomotives, V2 No 4771 was turned out of Doncaster Works in June 1936 and named *Green Arrow* which was the symbol of a newly-introduced registered express goods service. Given the standard apple-green passenger livery, the new locomotive looked very similar to the A3 class. In fact, it shared many features with the Pacific designs, the boiler being a shorter barrel version of the A3 and the cylinders of A4 pattern but with all three cast in one piece. The driving wheels were, however, 6 in smaller in diameter, but with internally streamlined steam passages and low clearance volumes the new locomotives soon showed themselves capable of high speed running well into the nineties. Other features included the Gresley 'banjo' shaped steam collector, V-shaped cab front, conjugate valve gear, one-piece forged piston and rod, nickel-chrome steel coupling and connecting rods, twin regulator handles, vertical screw reversing gear with vacuum lock, double-bolster swing-link pony truck and group standard six-wheeled tender with water scoop. In fact, it can be seen that in a single outstanding design virtually every feature was included that Gresley had found to be efficient and reliable in service, with

the possible omission of the Kylchap double blastpipe which was then still only in experimental use on the LNER. It was also a singularly handsome machine.

In accordance with the usual Gresley practice, the five original V2s were given extended trials before any further examples of the new class were built. *Green Arrow* went to Kings Cross and regularly worked the down 'Scotch Goods', the freight equivalent of the 'Flying Scotsman'. The next two were allocated to York, 4774 to Peterborough and the last of the batch to Dundee. On the Aberdeen road the V2 was rostered to take the same load as a Pacific and was accepted as a most useful and popular general purpose locomotive for this difficult route.

Twenty more V2s were built in 1937 with additional examples being added to stock each year thereafter until 1944, which saw the completion of the last five, making a total of 184. Actually there should have been 188, but Thompson modified the front-end design of the last four ordered and they were turned out as Pacifics classified A2/1.

Although restricted to some 43% of the LNER route mileage the V2s were to be found hard at work throughout the main line system and their performance on express passenger duties was virtually indistinguishable from the Pacifics. They excelled on the 'Yorkshire Pullman' with a 60 mph start to stop average between Kings Cross and Doncaster and load of 400 tons. No 4817 attained 93 mph on this train, covering $17\frac{1}{2}$ miles at an average speed of over 86 mph. There were even occasions when a V2

87 *Green Arrow* as it entered service and, except for the post-war fitted modified pony truck, as now preserved.

57

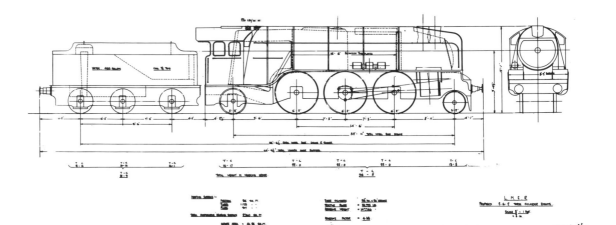

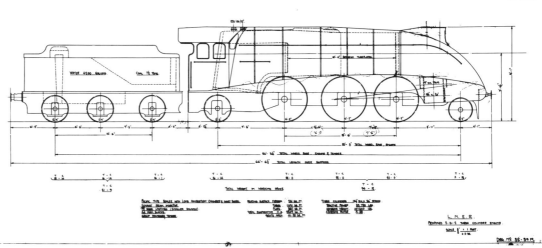

TYPE V2

88 1934 and 1935 outline schemes for the V2. The earlier version is very much a cut down *Cock o' the North* whilst the later one follows A4 practice. Both include double chimneys, a feature not fitted to some production locomotives until 1960.

89 On the duties for which specifically designed, *Green Arrow* leaves King's Cross with the down Scotch goods. An N2 and C1 awaits its passage at the exit signal from the running shed to proceed to the passenger station.
(C.C.B. Herbert)

58

was called upon to deputise for an A4 on one of the streamlined trains, proving that 6 ft 2 in diameter driving wheels were no handicap to sustained high-speed running when connected to an excellent front-end, even without the benefit of a Kylchap exhaust. On the GC main line some very fast running occurred with V2s and No 4830 was recorded as having averaged 80 mph for a total of 46½ miles with the 6.20 pm Marylebone to Leicester. On express freight work, particularly with the 'Scotch Goods', loads of over 600 tons were hauled at speeds in excess of 60 mph with ease.

By the end of 1939 there were 86 V2s in service. Being classed as mixed traffic locomotives they were not affected by the wartime ban on the construction of express passenger types and a further 32 were built in 1940. With over 100 Pacifics as well, the LNER was better supplied with high-capacity motive power for heavy wartime duties than any of the other three railway companies. The V2s were a great national asset during the war years, and worked extremely heavy passenger and freight trains. What is thought to be the heaviest express passenger-train ever worked in Britain, a 26-coach train of 850 tons gross weight carrying some 1300 passengers, was hauled by V2 No 4800 in March 1940 and loads in the 700–800

ton range became almost commonplace. A 20-coach load of 700 tons gross was worked from Newcastle to Grantham by No 4886 and gained 11 mins on the wartime schedule, sustaining a speed of over 60 mph for many miles between Darlington and York. On another wartime run with a load of 690 tons, No 4786 covered the 27 miles of generally adverse gradient between Huntingdon and Hitchin in 27½ mins. One unusual wartime V2 exploit was the working of an up express by No 4851 which maintained sectional timings from Retford to Grantham running tender first.

After the war most locomotives were suffering from years of overwork and neglect and the V2s were no exception. It was to be some years before the arrears of maintenance were made up and this applied in the other railway departments as well. In 1946 two V2s were involved in detailments on poor track and there was some criticism of the design of the swing-link pony truck. As a result, a new design of leading truck with spring-loaded side control was fitted. With better track conditions the V2s gradually returned to near pre-war standards of performance. In 1950, No 60889 working a 14-coach load of 510 tons gross ran the 31 miles from Knebworth to Offord at an average speed of 76½ mph with a maximum of 84 mph.

90 In early BR days, V2 No 60917 works 'The West Riding', which includes some of the 1937 built 'West Riding Limited; articulated stock.
(Rev. A.C. Cawston collection–NRM)

The fitting of the LMS type self-cleaning smokebox screens to some V2s had a disastrous effect on their steaming qualities as well as being unpopular with the boiler washing staff. One of those affected, No 60845, was sent to the Swindon Test Plant in an endeavour to rectify the situation. With relatively small alterations to the blastpipe it was found possible to double the steaming capacity from the very poor rate of 14,000lb/hr which was all the locomotive was capable of when received.

As built, the V2 was able to produce 31,000 lbs of steam per hour corresponding to an indicated horse power of 1990. At minimum steam consumption rates and working at 15% cut-off with a steaming rate of 20,000 lb/hr corresponding to 1510 IHP the V2 had a combined boiler and cylinder efficiency of 11.0. This was better than any of the BR standard designs, the LMS Duchess and Class 5, GWR King or SR Merchant Navy in original or rebuilt forms.

Towards the end of steam traction on British Railways, two V2s were fitted with the simple double blastpipe as used on some LMS and BR standard locomotives, but this seemed to effect only a very minor improvement in performance. More striking results were obtained by fitting the Kylchap arrangement to five locomotives. One of these was generally provided for the Peterborough Pilot turn and far too often was called upon to replace failed diesels. More than once loads of over 400 tons were worked to Kings Cross in under even time in these circumstances. To reduce repair and overhaul costs, three separate cylinders were fitted when the monoblock castings required renewal, the modified locomotives being easily recognisable by their outside steam pipes.

With their limited route availability the V2s did not normally venture far from the LNER main lines but they did stray further afield in post-war days. In 1953 problems with the Merchant Navy Pacifics caused them to be temporarily withdrawn from service and some V2s were drafted to the Southern Region. Trains worked by them on foreign territory included the West of England expresses and famous 'Bournemouth Belle'.

The V2s were regular visitors to the GWR at Banbury and in Scotland they became a fairly familiar sight on the former LMS main lines working both passenger and freight trains. On home ground, the short Alnmouth to Alnwick line was one of the last branch lines to have rostered steam worked passenger services. The class K1 2-6-0s were the regular performers in latter days, but Dundee V2 No 60836 worked the branch for a few days in May 1966 and the last day of steam operation the following month was covered by 9F 2-10-0 No. 92099.

Mileages of over 8000 a month were achieved by some of the Kings Cross V2s during the summer months. The Peterborough New England men certainly preferred their generally run-down examples to the BR Britannias and 9Fs. On the GC they were more popular than the rebuilt Royal Scots, which, it is only fair to add, only worked over the route in their final years.

The last V2 No 60836, was withdrawn from service in December 1966, nearly six years after the last of the Thompson 'improved' versions. Fortunately the pioneer *Green Arrow* was preserved and restored to LNER livery. Later it was put into working order and worked a number of special trains before being displayed in the National Railway Museum at York.

91 Class V2 No 60896 on loan to the Southern Region, heads *The Bournemouth Belle* at Waterloo on 20 May 1953. (R.C. Riley)

Appendix A

L.N.E.R. Tender and specification of 2-6-2 engines and tenders, class V-2

GENERAL CONDITIONS

The Engines must be in strict accordance with the terms of this Specification, and to the general and detailed description and dimensions given on drawings to be supplied by the London and North Eastern Railway Company's Chief Mechanical Engineer, hereinafter called the Chief Mechanical Engineer, except in cases where his consent to an alteration has been obtained in writing.

All materials used in the construction of these engines to be of British manufacture, and to be of the description and quality specified in each case, and where not defined, or instructions given, both workmanship and materials must be of the very best of their respective kinds.

Before any material is ordered, the Chief Mechanical Engineer shall have approved, in writing, the names of the Firms from whom the Contractor proposes to purchase, and after selection, he must be duly advised.

The words "Chief Mechanical Engineer" used in this specification shall be deemed to refer to the Chief Mechanical Engineer of the London and North Eastern Railway.

No advantage whatever is to be taken of any omission or discrepancy in the Drawings or Specification, or both, as the Chief Mechanical Engineer will supply all necessary information upon application, and fully explain any Points which may not be clearly shown or understood.

The Engines must be finished in every respect to the entire satisfaction of the Chief Mechanical Engineer, who shall at any and at all times during the progress of the work be at liberty to inspect the same, either personally or by deputy, and to reject anything which he or his deputy may consider deficient or defective, either as regards material or workmanship. All material used in manufacture, etc., must be supplied to London and North Eastern Railway Company's Specifications, except where otherwise stated, and must be tested in the presence of the Company's Inspector.

The Chief Mechanical Engineer reserves to himself the right of testing from time to time (as specified or by additional tests as he may elect) any portion of material used under this Contract either at the Contractor's Works, the Company's own Works, the work of any Firms supplying the materials to be used in the construction of these engines, or at any works (for testing purposes) which hereafter may be decided upon, and should any test not be to his entire satisfaction, he has the right to reject any or the whole of such material so tested, the entire cost of all tests, chemical or mechanical, which he may desire to make to be borne by the Contractor, including both cost of material and preparation of same for testing.

The Contractor to pay all royalties and patent rights.

The price named in the Tender is to include everything required to be done by the Conditions of the Contract, Specification and Drawings, and all such work as is necessary to the proper completion of the Contract notwithstanding that special mention thereof may have been omitted in the Specification or Drawings.

The Directors do not bind themselves to accept the lowest or any tender, and also reserve to themselves the right to divide the order amongst two or more firms as they think proper.

The engines throughout to be made to gauges and templates so as to be duplicates each of the other, and to ensure the various parts being interchangeable.

The engines to be delivered free of charge, fit and ready for work in all respects. The engines will be required to run 2,000 consecutive miles each without showing any defects in material or workmanship, and the Contractor will be responsible for all defects that may appear (accidents excepted) until they have run that distance.

Terms of Payment.
Fifty per cent. of Contract price per locomotive will be paid by the Company to the Contractors

61

on the erection of each engine after steaming of the boiler. A further 25 per cent. will be paid on delivery of each engine, and the balance of 25 per cent. will be paid after each engine has run two thousand (2,000) miles.

No payment is to become due or payable under this Contract without the written certificate of the Chief Mechanical Engineer.

In case of any dispute arising in connection with the construction of these engines, whether during the progress of Contract or at its termination, the decision of the Chief Mechanical Engineer is to be taken as final and binding in every respect.

Tracings, List of Materials, Photographs, Weights, etc.

If any alterations from the Drawings are agreed to, the Contractor is to provide the Chief Mechanical Engineer with tracings showing such alterations.

The Contractor is to provide the Company's Chief Mechanical Engineer with one complete set of Detailed and General tracings on cloth of uniform size together with two sets of black and white prints on cloth, each set to be bound in suitable and convenient sections, and indexed; and also two complete lists of all materials used in their construction, including the names of the firms from whom purchased, with the weights and sketches of all the details.

Patterns, Flanging Blocks and Templates.

The Contractor to provide all patterns and flanging blocks required.

The Contractor to send one set of steel and copper Firebox Wrapper Plates to the Company's works where they will be marked off, drilled and returned to the Contractor for use as templates.

The cost of conveyance and work on these plates to be borne by the Contractor.

Standard Allowances.

PINS: All Pins in plain joints to be made not more than standard size and not less than the standard size, minus $\cdot 002$ inch.

WORKING HOLES: All working holes to be made between $\cdot 003$ inch and $\cdot 005$ inch above the standard size.

FIXED PINS: In the case of the die and link, the die to be treated as a pin and the slot in link to have the clearance as for a pin hole.

SIDEWAY FITS: In the case of sideway fits, as in jaws, etc., the centre piece to be treated as a pin,

and the outside pieces to be made so as to give a total side allowance of from $\cdot 016$ inch to $\cdot 025$ inch above standard gauge width between.

BALL AND ROLLER BEARINGS: The tolerances of the pins and housings to be as specified on the drawings.

Bolts and Nuts.

All bolt heads, nuts and threads to be to Whitworth Standard Gauge.

All gland, steam chest cover and cylinder nuts to be case-hardened. Care must be taken to prevent the case-hardening extending to the threads. Horn-block bolts to be made of 3 per cent. nickel steel, heat-treated.

Joints.

All steam joints to be made metal to metal without the use of any other jointing medium than boiled oil, unless otherwise stated in the drawing.

Threads for Brasswork.

All brasswork up to and including $\frac{5}{8}$ inch diameter to Whitworth Standard Threads, above $\frac{5}{8}$ inch diameter 11 threads per inch except where stated otherwise on Drawings.

Tools, Spanners, Lamps, etc.

Each engine to be provided with a complete set of tools, firing-irons, oil bottles and feeders, head lamps, gauge lamps, etc., in accordance with List and Drawings.

Tool Boxes.

To be fitted as shown on Drawings.

Painting.

All ironwork to be thoroughly cleaned free from rust and grease.

The boiler to receive a coat of boiled oil on outside whilst hot, and one coat of Best Oxide paint when cooled down (see "Testing"). The inside of tanks to receive two coats of Best Oxide paint.

Lagging plates to have two coats of Lead colour inside.

The whole of the engine to be painted with one coat of Lead colour, all bad places and rivets stopped, then plastered all over with approved Enamel Filling, and afterwards rubbed down with pumice blocsk to a level surface.

Then to have two coats of Lead colour and two coats of L.N.E.R. Standard Green to panel supplied, picked out, lined and lettered to pattern and Drawing. Then to have three coats of varnish, flatted between each coat.

Frames on outside, footsteps, buffers, etc., to be painted black and lined to pattern.

Buffer plates to be Red and lined White to pattern.

Inside of frames, axles, injectors, ejectors, etc., to have one coat of Spirit Red and one coat of Varnish Red.

Engine wheels to be painted L.N.E.R. Standard Green and lined to pattern and varnished three coats, before being put under engine.

Brake Gear, Spring Gear, Ashpan, Footplate, etc., to have two coats of Japan Black.

Inside of cab and front of tender to be finished Dark Green and varnished three coats. Top of cab, outside, to be Japan Black.

Smokebox and chimney to have one coat Asbestos Black and one coat Japan Black.

Tender top and coal bunker to be Japan Black. The Company's initials, L.N.E.R., to be put on each side of the tender, the engine number on each side of the cab and engine number and classification on front buffer beam to drawing and pattern.

SPECIFICATION

Boiler and Firebox Shell.

Boiler and firebox shell, including all angles and rivets, to be made of Boiler steel to the form and dimensions shown on Drawings and to L.N.E.R. Specifications as follows:–

Plates to Specification No. 23.

Rivets and crown stays (except two outer rows) to Specification No. 26.

Barrel to be made in two plates, with flantged tubeplate as shown.

All longitudinal, palm and each outer row of crown stays to be of best Yorkshire iron, to L.N.E.R. Specification No. 41. All rivets must completely fill the holes, which must be drilled. All holes in the plates and angles must be slightly countersunk under the rivet heads, excepting where otherwise shown, the burrs to be filed off, and the holes must be perfectly fair with each other, **and no drifting will be allowed on any consideration whatever.**

Should any of the holes not come perfectly fair with each other, they must be carefully reamered until they become so. Care must be taken that, after reamering, the rivets completely fill the holes.

After all holes have been drilled and reamered, the plates must be taken apart and the joints thoroughly cleaned before being finally put together for riveting. All plates to be brought well together before any rivets are put in. All joints as far as possible must be fullered or caulked both inside and outside. Fullering must be done with a broad faced tool, care being taken that the plates are not damaged.

All Boiler plates and angles to be edge planed and suitably bevelled for fullering before being put together.

All joints, except that of the back plate of the firebox casing, to be riveted by hydraulic riveter with a pressure of 70 tons, with steel rivets as shown on the drawings.

The joint of the back plate to the casing plate to be hand-riveted in the presence of the Company's Inspector.

All flanged plates to be annealed after flanging.

The brand of the manufacturer of the plates to be kept where it can be seen.

A register to be taken of the numbers stamped on the copper fire-box and steel boiler plates used in the respective boilers.

The firebox foundation ring to be of the section shown on Drawings and made of forged steel to L.N.E.R. Specification No. 11, Class B.

Inside Firebox.

To be made of copper to L.N.E.R. Specification No. 16.

The plates to be planed up on both edges, and joints carefully caulked inside and out.

The stays on the sides, throat plate and door plate to be of copper to L.N.E.R. Specification No. 17A, and to be tightly screwed into plates and sawn off to length; to be hammered over with pneumatic hammer and round faced "bob" tool; the weight of the hammer not to exceed 12 lbs. with a piston $1\frac{1}{16}$ in. diameter by 3 in. stroke and an air pressure not less than 90 lbs. per square inch.

The rivets used in the copper box to be of best Yorkshire iron to L.N.E.R. Specification No. 41.

The stays must be tightly screwed into the copper and steel plates, care being taken to ensure tight fitting threads.

The stays to be strictly in accordance with Drawings, and the holes in both plates to be in perfect alignment with each other, and tapped with a long tap to ensure a continuous thread.

The copper stays, after having been placed in position, must not be riveted until each stay has been tested by the Company's Inspector.

The ends of the stays to be pneumatically riveted strictly in accordance with Drawing.

The tube holes, after being drilled in the copper tubeplate, must be reamered with a taper reamer having the taper similar to the tube expanders.

Tubes.

Steel boiler tubes and flues to L.N.E.R. Specification No. 20. Tubes to be secured to tube plates in the manner shown on Drawings.

Internal Pipes.

All internal pipes to be of copper to L.N.E.R. Specification No. 19. The main steam pipe to be stiffened with steel hoops, shrunk on as shown on Drawing.

Washout and Fusible Plugs.

To be of bronze to L.N.E.R. Standard Pattern.

Superheater.

The header and elements to be supplied by The Superheater Company, Limited. To be fitted with 43 elements and anti-vacuum valve as shown on drawings. The elements to be in accordance with L.N.E.R. Specification No. 20 and to have forged steel ends.

Injectors.

Supplied by approved Makers.

Ejector.

Supplied by approved Makers.

Testing.

The boiler before being clothed is to be tested in the presence of the Chief Mechanical Engineer or his deputy with the following tests. The boiler to receive a coat of boiled oil on outside whilst hot, and one coat of Best Oxide paint when cooled down. All fittings, studs, etc., to be in place before testing.

(A) HYDRAULIC TEST.

1. Test pressure to be not less than $1 \cdot 25 \times$ working pressure plus 10 lbs., nor more than $1 \cdot 5$ of the working pressure. Pressure to be maintained for not less than 10 minutes.

2. Hot water to be used.

3. Fullering or caulking may be done at pressures under 100 lbs. per square inch.

(B) STEAM TEST.

1. Test pressure to be equal to working pressure plus 10 lbs.

2. The time taken to raise steam to test pressure to be not less than two hours.

3. Full test pressure to be maintained for not less than one hour.

4. A second test need only be made in cases where it is found necessary.

5. Fullering or caulking may be done at pressures under 100 lbs. per square inch.

Boiler Clothing.

The Boiler barrel and dome to be clothed with Asbestos blocks and the firebox sides and crown to be clothed with Asbestos mattresses of approved make to L.N.E.R. Specification No. 55.

The insulation is to be covered with good quality mild steel sheets supported on crinoline hoops, and secured to the boiler and firebox with steel straps.

The firebox back is to be clothed with asbestos mill board covered by good quality mild steel sheets, and the whole arrangement to be to Drawing. All sheets to be perfectly level, sheets and bands to be of uniform thickness and to have a smooth planished surface. Handrails and pillars to be finished L.N.E.R. Standard Green.

Smokebox.

Plates to be of steel to L.N.E.R. Specification No. 25. Doors to be flanged, and to make a perfect joint on smokebox, with asbestos ring as shown on Drawing. All rivets on outside to be countersunk, and plates to be ground up smooth before bending. All nuts inside the smokebox to be made of hard bronze with solid end except where otherwise stated. The bottom to be floated with cement or ganister as shown on Drawing. Hand rails, pillars, etc. on smokebox to be finished black.

Chimney.

The chimney to be of cast iron to L.N.E.R. Specification No. 14, to the form and dimensions shown on Drawing, and to be carefully bedded to the smokebox.

Ash Pan.

To be of steel plates to L.N.E.R. Specification No. 25, fitted with dampers worked from the footplate as shown on the drawings. Firebars to be as shown on Drawing and to be a mixture of $12\frac{1}{2}\%$ steel and $87\frac{1}{2}\%$ cast iron scrap.

Main Frames.

The main frames to be of mild steel to L.N.E.R. Specification No. 24, the greatest care being taken to ensure the frames being of a uniform thickness throughout. They must be perfectly flat and free from cross windings and finished to a good surface for the attachment of the cylinders, stretchers, brackets, etc. All holes must be drilled from one template. The holes to be drilled under size and reamered to the exact size as shown on the Drawings, after the several details have been put together.

When the frames, cylinders, and motion plate have been fastened together, the accuracy of the work must be carefully checked by longitudinal, transverse, and diagonal measurements, and before final attachment the alignment must be passed by the Company's Inspector.

Hornblocks.

To be of Cast Steel to L.N.E.R. Specification No. 13, Class A for Castings with wearing surfaces. They must be accurately fitted and bedded to the frames, and secured by turned nickel steel bolts, a tight driving fit in reamered holes.

The Wedges to be of Cast Steel to L.N.E.R. Specification No. 13, Class A, with wearing surfaces.

Trailing Hornblocks to have Manganese Steel liners fitted to the faces as shown on the Drawing.

Axleboxes.

Axleboxes for Pony Truck and coupled wheels to be of bronze and lined as shown on Drawing.

Axleboxes for trailing carrying wheels to be of Cast Steel to L.N.E.R. Specification No. 13 Class A with wearing surfaces, fitted with bronze bearing lined as shown on Drawing. Manganese Steel liners to be fitted to the faces as shown on the Drawing.

Axlebox keeps to be fitted with "Armstrong" Pads to L.N.E.R. Specification No. 73.

Platform Plates.

To be of steel to L.N.E.R. Specification No. 25. To be carefully levelled and free from cross windings and secured as shown on Drawings.

The outside platform angle to be made of mild steel to L.N.E.R. Specification No. 27.

Sandboxes and Sandgear.

Sandboxes to be fabricated from mild steel plate to L.N.E.R. Specification No. 25. All sandgear to be made strictly in accordance with Drawings.

Buffers.

To be strictly in accordance with Drawing, and L.N.E.R. Specifications, and to be fitted with india-rubber springs as shown on Drawings.

Buffer Plates.

To be of mild steel to L.N.E.R. Specification No. 25, and fitted as shown on Drawing.

Cab.

Plates to be of steel to L.N.E.R. Specification No. 25, with rivets countersunk on outside. Windows, seats, wood-platform, number plate, tool box, handrails, doors, etc., to be provided as shown on Drawing. Handrails and pillars to be finished L.N.E.R. Standard Green.

Bearing Springs and Spring Gear.

Laminated springs to be to L.N.E.R. Specification No. 7 as shown on the Drawings.

The spring links and pins to be made of steel to L.N.E.R. Specification No. 11, Class A, with wearing surfaces carefully case-hardened. Helical Springs of pony truck to be made to L.N.E.R. Specification No. 9, and to be of "Timmis" section. India-rubber auxiliary springs to be provided as shown on Drawing. The spring brackets for the coupled wheels are to be steel castings to L.N.E.R. Specification No. 13, Class A (for castings without wearing surfaces.)

Cylinders.

The cylinders to be of cast-iron, to L.N.E.R. Specification No. 14. They must be accurately bored and bell-mouthed, as shown on the Drawing. Care must be taken that all thicknesses are regular in barrels, ports and passages. All joints and surfaces to be planed or turned and scraped to a true surface, so that perfectly steam-tight joints can be obtained without any other jointing medium than boiled oil. They are to be tested in the presence of the Company's Inspector by hydraulic pressure of 300 lbs. per square inch.

All gland, steam chest cover and cylinder nuts to be case-hardened.

Piston Valve Liners.

The piston valve liners to be of similar metal to the cylinders.

Blast Pipe.

To be of cast iron to L.N.E.R. Specification No. 14, as shown on Drawing. The base of pipe to be accurately faced to form joint with flange on cylinder casting.

Piston Valve Spindles.

To be made of steel to L.N.E.R. Specification No. 11, Class D, accurately fitted to the valve heads as shown on Drawing.

Piston Valves and Rings.

Piston Valve Heads and Rings to be made of cast iron to L.N.E.R. Specification No. 14 (Cylinder Mixture) and Drawings.

Combined Pistons and Rods.

Combined Pistons and rods to be forged solid of steel to L.N.E.R. Specification No. 11, Class C.

Piston rings to be made of cast iron to L.N.E.R. Specification No. 14 (Cylinder Mixture) and Drawings.

Rod Packing.

The piston rods to be fitted with cast iron packing and the valve spindles with white metal packing in accordance with the Drawings.

Crossheads.

Crosshead to be of cast steel to L.N.E.R. Specification No. 13, Class A, and Drawing, faced with anti-friction metal, as shown on Drawing. The gudgeon pins to be forged of steel to L.N.E.R. Specification No. 11, Class D.

Motion Bars.

To be forged steel to L.N.E.R. Specification No. 11, Class D. To be accurately machined and secured to the cylinders and motion plates as shown on Drawings.

Valve Motion.

All motion work (except the large motion lever) to be forged of steel to L.N.E.R. Specification No. 11, Class A. All working surfaces to be carefully case-hardened and re-heated before quenching.

Large motion lever to be of steel to L.N.E.R. Specification No. 11, Class C.

The Ball and Roller Bearings must be fitted with great accuracy.

The whole to be finished strictly in accordance with the Drawings.

Reversing Gear.

Screw reversing gear graduated for expansion to be fitted as shown on Drawing.

The reversing shaft and reversing shaft arms to be of Mild Steel to L.N.E.R. Specification No. 11, Class A.

Motion Plate.

The motion plates to be cast steel to L.N.E.R. Specification No. 13, Class A, without wearing surfaces, and to be carefully machined to suit the frames, and secured as shown on Drawing.

Connecting and Coupling Rods.

To be of Nickel Chrome Molybdenum Steel heat treated to L.N.E.R. Specification No. 43.

All roads to be first machined as shown on drawings and then sent to the makers for heat treatment. Afterwards they are to be machined to the finished sizes and finished complete as shown on the drawings.

The large end strap for the inside connecting rod to be made of Class 3 Tyre Steel "B" to L.N.E.R. Specification No. 28.

Wheels.

To be of cast steel to L.N.E.R. Specification No. 13, Class B, and Drawings. To be perfectly free from honeycomb.

Each wheel boss must be accurately bored out and the wheel seat turned smooth and parallel. The hole in the boss and the axle wheel seat to be coated with pure rape oil as lubricant, and the wheel forced on to its seat by hydraulic power with a pressure of not less than 10 tons or more than 12 tons per inch diameter of wheel seat. The machine by which wheels are pressed on must be fitted with an approved automatic recorder, and the records, numbered to correspond with the wheels, to be delivered to the Chief Mechanical Engineer.

Tyres.

Tyres for the coupled wheels to be of steel to L.N.E.R. Specification No. 4, Class C, and the tyres for the pony truck and trailing wheels to be to L.N.E.R. Specification No. 4, Class D.

The tyres of the coupled, pony truck, and trailer carrying wheels to be bored with a shrinkage allowance of $\frac{1}{820}$, $\frac{1}{972}$, and $\frac{1}{941}$ of the inside diameter respectively. Wheel centres to be turned to the dimensions on Drawings, and the tyres to be bored smaller by the amount of the shrinkage required.

The shrinkage of tyres to be checked by measurements taken with a steel tape over a cylindrically turned portion of the tread, before and after shrinking on the wheel centres.

Crank Pins.

To be made of steel to L.N.E.R. Specification No. 11, Class D. The crank pins to be forced into wheels by hydraulic pressure of not less than 10 tons per inch diameter and the end riveted over into a countersunk recess. Taper of pin to be as shown on Drawing.

The crank pin washers to be made of steel to L.N.E.R. Specification No. 11, Class D. The washers are to be screwed on to the ends of the crank pins and the taper split pins, securing them to the pins, must have their larger ends towards the centre of the wheels.

Axles.

The built-up crank and straight axles to be made of steel to L.N.E.R. Specification Nos. 42 and 2, respectively. The axles must be machined all over and burnished on the bearings.

The webs of the crank axles are to be machined in pairs, and the bores are to be machined out and carefully ground to standard diameter while the edges of the webs are perfectly level. In the event of the webs being cut by oxy-acetylene an allowance of $\frac{1}{2}$ in. must be left for machining. The crank pin is to be finished machined and ground on the web seats with an allowance of plus $\cdot$018.

The shafts are to be machined with an allowance for finishing on the wheel seats and journals after assembly. The web seats on the shafts are to be finished by grinding with an allowance of plus $\cdot$018.

The webs must be heated by gas ring, in which the jets are disposed equally round the whole perimeter of the web, until the pins and shafts pass freely in to the holes.

Suitable allowances must be made during assembly to ensure that the shaft and pin ends come flush with the web after cooling down, and that the webs come perfectly parallel with each other.

After assembly the axle is to be trued up on the journals and on the wheel seats.

The tonnage at which the wheels are pressed on the axles to be clearly stamped thereon.

Brake Gear.

The engine is to be fitted with vacuum brake and as shown on Drawings. Brake fittings to be supplied by approved makers and the whole arrangements to be to Drawing. Brake hangers, beams, rods and shaft to be made of steel to L.N.E.R. Specification No. 11, Class A. bushed as shown on Drawing. All copper tubing in connection with the brake work must be solid drawn.

Draw Gear.

Draw hooks, screw couplings, and shackles to be made of steel without weld to L.N.E.R. Specification No. 34. All to be arranged as shown on Drawings.

Draw gear to be fitted with india-rubber springs as shown on Drawings.

Lubricators.

The steam chest, cylinder barrels and coupled axle boxes to be mechanically lubricated as shown on the Drawings.

Type of Lubricators to be approved by the Chief Mechanical Engineer.

Leading Pony Truck.

Truck and Radial Arm to be strictly in accordance with Drawings.

Truck frames to be of steel to L.N.E.R. Specification No. 24 and to be of a uniform thickness throughout, perfectly flat and free from cross windings.

The pony truck swing link pins to be grease lubricated, strictly in accordance with the Drawing.

Trailing Carrying Wheels.

The Axlebox Tops to be fitted with slides on the Cartazzi principle as shown on the Drawings.

Steam Heating.

Pipes, hose, and all necessary fittings to be supplied as shown on Drawings.

TENDER.

The top, sides, ends and platform plates to be made of steel to L.N.E.R. Specification No. 25 and in accordance with Drawing. The angles, stays, fill-hole and other fittings to be arranged as shown on Drawings.

All rivets, except where otherwise shown, to be countersunk outside and filed smooth.

Tank to be fixed to platform by angles and rivets and the whole to be firmly riveted to main frames, as shown on Drawings.

Manhole and water gauge to be fitted on tank as shown on Drawings.

Alternatively the tender, tank and platform, complete with water scoop pipe and filling hole may be constructed by electric welding.

The lifting eyes and lamp irons must be riveted as shown on the Drawings and the handrail secured in the usual manner.

Tender Main Frames.

To be of steel to L.N.E.R. Specification No. 24, rolled in one plate, the greatest care to be taken to ensure the frames being of uniform thickness throughout. All holes to be marked from one template and drilled and reamered to exact size given. When the frames are in position the accuracy of the work must be carefully tested by diagonal longitudinal and transverse measurements.

Frames to be finished with a good smooth surface and they must be true and free from cross windings. Inside stretcher plates to be of cast steel and secured to main frames, buffer beams, etc., as shown on Drawings.

Footsteps to be arranged as shown.

Rubbing Blocks.

Rubbing blocks to be fitted between engine and tender as shown on Drawings.

Draw Gear.

The intermediate drawbar, safety links, drawbook, screw coupling and shackles to be made of steel without weld to L.N.E.R. Specification No. 34. All to be arranged as shown on Drawings.

Tender Axles-boxes.

To be of cast iron to L.N.E.R. Specification No. 14, general castings, fitted with bronze bearings lined in accordance with the Drawings supplied.

Axle-box Guides.

To be of cast iron to L.N.E.R. Specification No. 14, general castings, to be finished perfectly true and parallel and to be perfectly square with the frames and finished to Drawing.

Bearing Springs.

To be in accordance with Drawing and to L.N.E.R. Specification No. 7.

Spring Links.

To be made of steel to L.N.E.R. Specification No. 11 Class "A" soundly forged and fitted with rubber pads, with covers as shown on Drawings.

Drag Box.

Front and hind drag box to be of cast steel to L.N.E.R. Specification No. 13, Class "A," for castings without wearing surfaces, and to be fitted as shown on Drawings.

Buffers.

To be as shown on Drawing, and to L.N.E.R. Specifications, and to be fitted with india-rubber springs, as shown on Drawings.

Wheel and Axles.

To be to L.N.E.R. Specification No. 72. Disc wheel centres to be to L.N.E.R. Specification No. 38.

Tyres.

To be of steel to L.N.E.R. Specification No. 4, Class "D."

Axles.

To be of steel to L.N.E.R. Specification No. 2.

Brake Gear.

To be in accordance with Drawing. The brake hangers, beams, rods and shaft to be made of steel to L.N.E.R. Specification No. 11, Class "A" with wearing surface bushed as shown on Drawing.

Angles.

To be of mild steel to L.N.E.R. Specification No. 27.

Water Scoop.

Water Pick-up apparatus to be fitted complete as shown on the Drawings supplied.

Steam Heating.

Pipes, hose, and all necessary fittings to be supplied as shown on Drawings.

A.R.P.

Cab roof and tender weather-board to be drilled for A.R.P. anti-glare screens.

H. N. GRESLEY,
Chief Mechanical Engineer.

London & North Eastern Railway Co., H.Q. 2, Watton House, Hertford.

Composition of Bronzes and White Metals to be pigged before casting.

BRONZES.	MIXTURE.	PURPOSE.
Copper	86.25%	Hard Metal for Axle boxes and all
Tin	13.25%	Bushes and Bearings. A suitable
Phosphor	0.5%	De-Oxidising agent to be used
Bronze		when Casting.
Copper	84%	For Boiler Mountings and
Tin	7%	General Small Castings.
Lead	4.5%	
Zinc	4.5%	
Copper	90%	Brazing Metal For Pipe Flanges
Zinc	10%	and Pipe Cones.

WHITE METALS.

Locomotive White
Bronze
"C" Quality supplied by
The Anti-Attrition
Metal Co.,
1, Victoria Street, Westminster, S.W.1.

Axlebox Bearings, Slideblocks,
Pony Truck Axlebox and Big End
Bearings.

or

STONES WHITE BRONZE
Supplied by–
J. Stone & Co., Oceanic House,
1A, Cockspur Street, London, S.W.1.

Lead   80.0%   Valve Spindle Packing Rings.
Antimony   20.0%

SUMMARY OF L.N.E.R. SPECIFICATIONS

Loco' and Tender, Straight Axles to be to L.N.E.R. Specification	No. 2, Feb., 1930
Loco' and Tender Tyres to be to L.N.E.R. Specification	No. 4, Feb., 1930
Laminated Springs	No. 7, Oct., 1932
Helical Springs	No. 9, Oct., 1932
Steel Forgings	No. 11, April, 1933
Steel Castings	No. 13, Mar., 1931
Iron Castings	No. 14, Jan., 1928
Copper Plates	No. 16, Feb., 1925
Copper Rods	No. 17A, Oct., 1935
Copper Pipes	No. 19, May, 1925
Steel Tubes	No. 20, April, 1927
Steel Boiler Plates	No. 23, Feb., 1930
Steel Plates for Loco' and Tender Frames	No. 24, Feb., 1930
Steel Plates for General Purposes	No. 25, Feb., 1930
Steel Sections and Bars for Loco' Boilers	No. 26, June, 1937
Steel Angles, etc., for General purposes	No. 27, Mar., 1930
Steel Bars, Ordinary Mill Finish	No. 28, Feb., 1930
Drawgear	No. 34, August, 1939
Steel Disc Centres	No. 38, Nov., 1932
Best Yorkshire Iron	No. 41, August, 1939
Built-up Crank Axles	No. 42, Nov., 1930
Nickel Chrome Molybdenum Forgings	No. 43, June, 1937
Asbestos Clothing for Locomotives	No. 55, July, 1936
Tender Wheels and Axles	No. 72, July, 1926
Axlebox Lubricators	No. 73, Sept., 1932

LIST OF TOOLS

1 Double Ended Spanner, $\frac{7}{8}$ in. $\times$ $\frac{3}{4}$ in.
1 Double Ended Spanner, 1 in. $\times$ $\frac{5}{8}$ in. (approximately 12 in. long and not more than $\frac{1}{4}$ in. thick).
1 Double Ended Spanner, $\frac{3}{8}$ in. $\times$ $\frac{1}{2}$ in.
1 Double Ended Ring Spanner, 1 in. $\times$ $1\frac{1}{8}$ in.
1 Pin Punch, small.
1 Monkey Spanner.
1 Coal Hammer.
1 Heavy Hammer.
1 Hand Hammer.
1 Lead Hammer.
1 Flat Chisel.
1 Pinch Bar.
1 Firing Shovel.
1 Clinker Shovel.
1 Pricker.
1 Rake.
1 Dart.
1 Tube Scraper.
1 Hand Lamp.
4 Head Lamps.
1 Gauge Lamp.
2 Torch Lamps.
1 8-pint Oil Bottle.
1 Water Bucket–2 gallons capacity.
1 9-in. Spouted 1-pint Oil Feeder.
1 Long Oil Feeder.
2 1-quart Tallow or Thick Oil Feeder.
1 16-pint Oil Bottle.
1 4-pint Oil Bottle.
1 Hand Brush.
2 Fog Signal Boxes.
Padlocks and Keys for all Toolboxes.
1 Grease Gun.

V-2 CLASS ENGINES

The following is a list of drawings accompanying this Specification for tendering purposes:–

Diagram of Engine and Tender

General Arrangement of Engine	P–77
Cylinders	M–533
Valve Gear Arrangement	K–424
Boiler	N–842
Engine Frame	O–253
Arrangement of Vacuum Brake on Tender	R–282
Tender Frame	R–290
Tender Tank	R–266

Fabricated alternatives of certain selected iron and steel castings, to facilitate early delivery will be considered.

7

Rebuilds

So far, we have looked at the work of Stanier and Gresley largely from the standpoint of designs which they originated, but it is wrong to assess the merits of an engineer solely on this criterion. Many of the greatest engineers owe their fame to the success with which they have improved upon the work of their predecessors. Perhaps the most outstanding example of the truth of this statement is to be found in the work of the famous French engineer André Chapelon who, so far as the French Railways were concerned, never actually designed a completely new locomotive. Even his immortal 242A1 was a rebuild.

If Gresley and Stanier cannot quite match Chapelon in this respect, their record of rebuilding older types is still very interesting. This is particularly true in the case of Gresley

who, faced with the financial constraints put upon him by the LNER in its early days, was frequently forced to rebuild because the money was not available for new construction. Stanier's company took a different view. The LMS felt that although rebuilding might be cheaper in the short run, new construction of a limited number of types embodying all the refinements designed to produce cheaper running and maintenance costs, showed medium to long term advantages. Thus, although Stanier refinements were applied to many of the older designs (e.g. the main production batch of Patriots), genuine rebuilding as such, was rarer than on the LNER.

Space precludes us from itemising all the possible examples of Gresley's and Stanier's work on older types of locomotives, but two particular cases do seem to warrant attention – the 1500 Class 4–6–0s of the GER and the Royal Scot 4–6–0s of the early LMS period. We choose these two, partly because they tend to give the lie to some cherished 'folk-myths' about these two men, in particular that Gresley was a 'three-cylinder' engineer and that Stanier eschewed this cylinder arrangement.

The Great Eastern Railway S69 or 1500 class 4–6–0s, introduced at the end of 1911, were particularly interesting locomotives in both concept and subsequent history. Designed under the nominal direction of S.D. Holden, but very much a product of Stratford drawing office, they had to meet very severe limitations in weight and length. As a result they were one of the smaller British 4–6–0s, with 6 ft 6 in diameter driving wheels, a maximum axle load of 15 tons 13 cwt and total wheelbase of 48 ft 3 in to permit turning on a 50 ft turntable. A 5 ft 1 in diameter boiler with 180 psi working pressure and

92 The first British locomotive to be fitted with Poppet valve gear. Class J20 0–6–0 No 8280 in 1925.

Belpaire firebox, supplied superheated steam to two 20 in × 28 in inside cylinders, giving a tractive effort of 21,969 lb. The 10 in piston valves with short travel were operated by Stephenson valve gear through rocking levers and the usual GE single slide bar was retained. Westinghouse air brakes were fitted and advantage was taken of the resultant compressed air supply to provide air-operated reversing gear, water scoop and sanding apparatus. Two somewhat unusual features were the $1\frac{1}{2}$ in controlled side play allowed on the trailing coupled axleboxes and the extension of the cab

floor over the tender drag box – an arrangement repeated 40 years later on the BR Britannia Pacifics.

Although little more powerful than a number of contemporary 4-4-0s, the 1500s must have looked quite magnificent in their original livery of dark blue with scarlet lining and polished brass work. In service, they put up some very creditable performances, particularly on the 'Hook Continental', and the GER added 71 to stock, although one was soon 'lost' in the Colchester collision of 1913. Following persistent trouble with the driving axle boxes, a change was

93 Ex-GER '1500' Class 4-6-0 No 8516 after fitting with Lenz oscillating Cam Poppet valve gear in 1926.

94 No 8571, first of ten Beyer–Peacock 1928 built B12s with Lenz valves, but minus some of the distinctive GER features.

made to the crank settings, from the conventional to the Stroudley arrangement whereby the coupling rod pin is in phase with the adjacent crank pin. This had the desired effect and the original locomotives were altered accordingly.

Becoming LNER class B12 after the grouping, they were probably the most generally successful, if by no means the largest, of the 4-6-0s inherited by the East Coast group. As such they continued to be the mainstay of the GE section express passenger services until 1928 when the three-cylinder B17 class appeared on the scene.

Somewhat surprisingly in view of the imminent arrival of the new locomotives, ten more B12s were ordered from Beyer-Peacock for

delivery in 1928. They incorporated a number of relatively minor modifications to the original GE design losing some of the special fittings, but the major change was the substitution of Lenz poppet valves operated by oscillating cams.

It was to a GE design that the first application of the German Lenz oscillating cam poppet valve gear was made in Britain. In 1925, locomotive No 8280 of class J20, at that time the most powerful 0-6-0 type in the country, had been experimentally fitted to see if the manufacturer's claims of better steam distribution and fuel economy were justified. As a result of the initial experience it was decided to extend the range of the trials and B12 No 8516 was similarly equipped the following year. Compared with an original piston valve locomotive with short travel valve gear, No 8516 showed a coal economy of some 9% on a train mile and 11% on a ton mile basis. It was these results which caused the specification for the Beyer-Peacock B12s to be amended to include Lenz valves.

Unfortunately, the early promise of a new development often fails to provide the hoped for long-term overall advantages and this was the case with the Lenz valve B12s. The locomotive performance was generally improved, with particularly good acceleration and free running at speed, but the overall fuel economy was not as good as expected. More serious was trouble with the cam shafts and cracking of the cylinder castings.

95 The disfigurement caused by the fitting of ACFI feed water heater is very apparent in this view of No 8519.

96 The first Gresley Class B17 4-6-0, No 2800 *Sandringham.* Specifically designed for the GE section, they differed from most Gresley designs in having divided drive and the 2-1 lever behind the cylinders.

Cylinder renewals are an expensive item and it was this factor which led to the decision to abandon the oscillating valve gear.

The B12s also featured in another extended trial which had a very adverse effect on the appearance of those involved and earned them the nickname of 'Camels'. Gresley conducted various experiments with waste heat recovery apparatus, the ACFI feed water heater being the equipment most extensively used. In all, 55 B12s were fitted with the heater which was claimed to effect a 10% saving in coal and 15% in water consumption. It was found in practice, however, that the fuel and water economies were insufficient to justify the initial cost of the equipment and its maintenance, and a decision was taken in 1937 to remove the apparatus when new boilers were fitted. However, some of the locomotives had feed water heaters for up to ten years.

When the decision was made to abandon the Lenz valve gear, Stratford modified one of the piston valve locomotives No 8559 by making the valve gear rocking-lever arm lengths unequal and thus increasing the valve travel from $4\frac{3}{16}$ in to $6\frac{1}{16}$ in. Experience with this locomotive and improvements to the permanent way in East Anglia made it possible to undertake a more extensive rebuilding of the B12 class. The detail design work was undertaken at Stratford under the general direction of Edward Thompson, but it was very much a Gresley locomotive which resulted.

Classified B12/3, the rebuilds were fitted with a larger boiler of Gresley pattern and a redesigned front end. The new boiler was 5 ft 6 in diameter with a round top firebox and larger superheater, similar to, but not interchangeable with, the B17 type. A completely new valve gear, but still of the Stephenson type, was fitted, giving a maximum valve travel of $6\frac{1}{16}$ in. It was so arranged that at 15% cut-off the opening to exhaust equalled the full width of the ports. Although the piston valve diameter was reduced from 10 in to $9\frac{1}{2}$ in, the original cylinder casting was retained. As the boiler pressure and cylinder dimensions remained unaltered there was no increase in tractive effort, but the maximum axle load went up to 17 tons and the adhesive weight to 48 tons 2 cwt.

The B12/3s were an immediate and lasting success, and between 1932 and 1944 all the Lenz valve examples, together with the piston valve locomotives remaining in England, 54 in all, were rebuilt accordingly. The improved front end resulted in a 20% saving in coal and water consumption compared with the original GER design. In the late 1930s, the down 'Hook Continental' loading to 465 tons was regularly rostered to a B12/3. On the Norwich route speeds of 90 mph were recorded with them and they were probably the best riding 4–6–0 ever

97 With his 1932 rebuild, Gresley produced an even more attractive and certainly more efficient design than the original GER version. B12/3 No 8579.

built. During the Second World War they were regularly called upon to work trains of weights approaching 500 tons. Being fitted for working both air and vacuum braked trains and having a wide route availability with their low axle load, they were a most useful 'wartime duties' locomotive and worked the American forces ambulance trains over the 'other companies' lines, particularly in the South West.

After the war they continued on main line duties in East Anglia, also working on the M & GN and from Grantham and Peterborough Spital depots over the former GNR and LNWR lines. It was from Grantham in 1950 that No 61553 worked the 14 coach up 'West Riding' unaided through to Kings Cross after an A3 had failed.

The last B12/3 No 61572 was withdrawn in September 1961 and is now happily preserved on the North Norfolk Railway.

Although having little more in common than wheel arrangement, the little B12/3 was just as successful a rebuild as the large 6P Royal Scot. It also provided an excellent example of how locomotive modernisation at a relatively low cost could enable a basically sound design to remain on main line duties for a period of 50 years.

While the Gresley rebuilds were showing their paces in East Anglia, the new Royal Scots were beginning to make their presence felt on the LMS system. Designed in a great hurry to meet an urgent need, their origins can be traced to an LMS/GWR locomotive exchange in 1926 when *Launceston Castle* proved as big an

embarrassment to the LMS as had *Pendennis Castle* to the LNER a year earlier. The difference was that unlike the LNER, the LMS had no suitable big engine to which the Swindon principles could be applied, although a 4-6-2 design was in the planning stage.

The main result of these trials was to convince the LMS management that a big 4-6-0 could do the job and the proposed 4-6-2 was therefore shelved. Rumour has it that the LMS tried to borrow the GWR Castle drawings from Swindon, but on being rebuffed, drew up a big three-cylinder design in great haste and ordered 50 straight off the drawing board in 1927. Although built by the North British Locomotive Company, the design emanated from Derby and perpetuated all the good front end features of the Horwich 2-6-0 and the Fowler 2-6-4T. The boiler probably owed something to the Southern Railway 'Lord Nelson' type but the three-cylinder layout was devised by the LMS and by the time Stanier arrived on the scene, the class had settled down to some prodigious haulage feats on the West Coast route.

During the early 1930s, the Royal Scots bore the brunt of LMS heavy express duties until the Stanier Pacifics began to come into service in larger numbers from 1935 onwards. Unfortunately, one or two features of the Royal Scot design caused the fuel consumption and maintenance costs to increase rapidly as mileage built up after each major overhaul. Many smaller detail improvements (axleboxes, piston rings etc.) could be made by Stanier to improve

98 B12/3 No 8517 heads an up stopping train out of Cambridge. (G.H. Soole collection – NRM)

matters, but the particular feature which could not easily be altered was the Derby type of built-up smokebox which was nothing like as good, or as trouble free as Stanier's Swindon type smokebox. This was made as a true cylinder and mounted on a separate saddle and was far more air-tight than the Derby variety. The Royal Scots were too valuable to permit wholesale withdrawal for attention to this matter even had authorisation been given to do so, so they had to soldier on for a few more years.

Eventually, when the original boilers fell due for replacement during World War II,

authorisation was given for a complete rebuild of the Royal Scots and this process commenced in 1943. Although the operation largely took place during the periods of office of Stanier's successors, Fairburn and H.G. Ivatt (son of the famous H.A. Ivatt of the GNR), the rebuilt or converted Royal Scots were in the by now classic Stanier tradition. All the development work had taken place during his term of office and these conversions can genuinely be referred to as Stanier engines.

Two main influences were brought together in the design. The 'prototype' for the rebuilt Scots was the quasi-experimental No 6170 *British Legion* built by Stanier in 1935. This engine was a rebuild of an experimental high pressure compound 4–6–0 No 6399 *Fury* whose boiler had 'exploded' with fatal results in 1929. The experiment was discontinued and Stanier used the frames and wheels as an opportunity to build a 4–6–0 with taper boiler larger than that used on the 5XP Jubilee class.

The resulting engine was a singularly handsome 'one-off' and quickly established a reputation as a swift and strong machine. Even so, although it did not repeat some of the earlier Stanier mistakes, it did need several adjustments to the front end (including alterations to the valve and steam port dimensions and the fitting of a double chimney), before becoming a very good performer indeed by 1937. However, it did not attract much notice at the time because of the publicity surrounding the new Coronation

99 The original Royal Scot design as built – No 6161 *King's Own*, one of the final 20 to be constructed. Unusually, this batch was built at Derby.

100 Parallel boiler Royal Scot No 6152 *The King's Dragoon Guardsman* in final configuration with smoke deflectors and Stanier tender. This engine was the original No 6100 having exchanged identities (permanently) with No 6152 when the latter was specially modified for the Royal Scot tour of America and Canada in 1933 and took the 6100 identity.

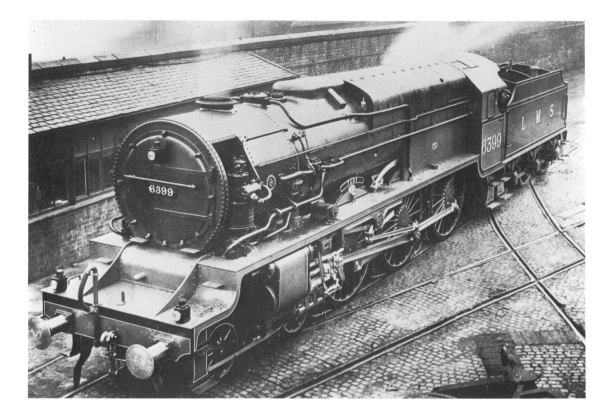

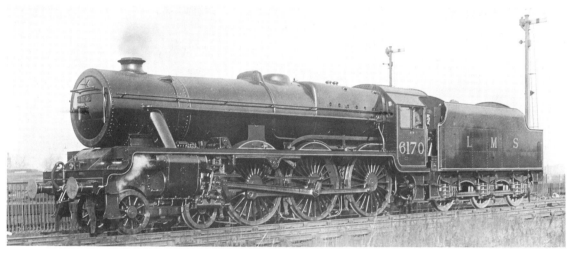

101/102 & 103 Evolution of the prototype rebuilt Scot. Experimental high pressure compound 4–6–0 No 6399 *Fury* was rebuilt in 1935 to the handsome No 6170, later named *British Legion.* By BR days, as No 46170, it had received smoke deflectors and double chimney, but the Stanier cab was always unique to this member of the class. (103, J.R. Carter)

104 No 6121 'H.L.I.' represents the rebuilt Scots in their common LMS form – without smoke deflectors. Note the retention of the Fowler Cab on an otherwise 'pure' Stanier design.

105 No 46100 *Royal Scot* did not achieve rebuilt status until BR days during the 1950s. This view shows it in the only colour scheme is ever carried in service – BR green. As preserved at Bressingham it is incorrectly painted in LMS crimson.

Pacifics. Nevertheless, Stanier had another potential winner on his hands.

There the matter may have rested but for the second major influence. By the late 1930s, both Gresley and Stanier were coming markedly under the influence of Chapelon, in particular in the realm of internal streamlining of the steam ports and passages, which was put to good effect both in the Stanier Coronation and the Gresley A4s. Stanier's chief designer, Tom Coleman, was particularly interested in these aspects and still not being wholly satisfied with the performance of the Jubilees, obtained permission from Stanier to produce a more powerful version, embodying all this newly acquired knowledge. Two Jubilees were therefore rebuilt with larger boilers, modified cylinders and valves, better bogie control and numerous other refinements. When the first of them entered service in 1942, it could out-perform not only the other 5XPs but the Royal Scots as well. Its general proportions were very similar to *British Legion* although because of slight dimensional differences in the engine chassis, *British Legion*'s boiler was not interchangeable with the 1942 version.

The general reboilering of the Jubilees could not yet be justified financially, but the Royal Scots did qualify for attention and it was the rebuilt Jubilee design of boiler and cylinders which was used for the Royal Scot conversion. Nationalisation prevented the application of this rebuilding process to the other LMS 4–6–0 classes except for a few of the parallel boiler Patriots.

Although classed as rebuilds, the converted Royal Scots were in most respects brand new machines and in this form they proved to be what most commentators agree was Britain's finest express passenger 4–6–0 type. During the 1948 interchange trials they put up performances which outclassed the GWR Kings and their drawbar horsepower fully matched that of most 4–6–2s involved in these trials. If they had a fault, it was that of rough riding when ready for shopping, but their haulage ability was always formidable, their fuel economy was good and, on occasion, they were timed at 100 miles per hour.

To the authors it was particularly pleasing to see these fine machines working turn and turn about with the 'Chapelonised' Gresley A3s on the Leeds–Carlisle main line during the final years of steam. It seemed nicely symbolic that the Leeds men, who had to drive both types, were prepared to accept the Gresley engines; a generation earlier the ex-LNWR Claughtons were not at all well received as a stable companion for a Midland Compound. Of course it could have been that the A3s were more comfortable than the Royal Scots–but we refuse to be drawn into that argument!

Two rebuilt Scots survive in preservation, both happily in working order. No 6115 *Scots Guardsman* is preserved in its correct final LMS condition and livery while No 6100 *Royal Scot* has been restored to its pre-war LMS red colours although its present external configuration dates from the mid-1950s.

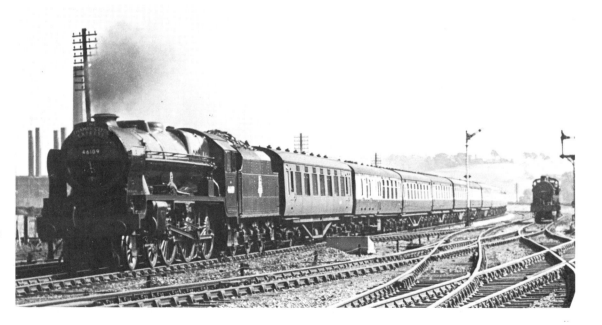

106 The rebuilt Scots first exhibited their potency on the Leeds–Carlisle line. One of Holbeck's famous examples, No 46109 *Royal Engineer* is seen here passing Kirkstall power station with the down "Thames–Clyde Express" in August 1952. (D. Jenkinson)

8

Built for power and speed

For the most part, when comparing work of Stanier and Gresley, it is not possible to match like with like, for the two men were usually working to rather different terms of reference. It was only in the realm of high speed higher performance passenger haulage that the two men both designed locomotives of broadly comparable proportions. Significantly, it was in this department that both produced what are generally considered to be their individual finest designs, each of which was supreme in its own field. The Gresley A4 was Britain's (and the world's) fastest ever steam locomotive, while the Stanier 'Princess Coronation' type, although nominally less powerful than Gresley's P2 class

2–8–2, proved itself capable of sustaining higher power outputs than any other British passenger steam design.

The streamlined A4 class Pacifics were designed to work the 'Silver Jubilee' train which, on entering service in September 1935, provided a four-hour service with one intermediate stop between London and Newcastle. The booked overall average speed of 71 mph between Darlington and London was to be achieved by fast up-hill running rather than by extra high speeds on falling gradients. This entailed an average running speed of 80–90 mph after allowing for starting, stopping and speed restrictions.

Had the German builders of the railcar used on the 'Flying Hamburger' been able to match these requirements, it is quite likely the A4s would never have been built, but they were unable to promise a higher average speed over the LNER main line than 63 mph. Sir Ralph Wedgewood, Chief General Manager of the LNER, suggested that rather than purchase the diesel rail car with its limited and cramped passenger accommodation compared with the spacious comfort of East Coast stock, a standard Pacific could better meet the needs in every respect. The well-publicised trial with *Papyrus* working a six-coach train when a maximum speed of 108 mph was attained, and the journey from Newcastle covered in 38 mins less than the German proposal, proved him to be correct. Even so, it was felt that economy in working and a greater margin of power would result if both locomotive and train were streamlined.

107 The first of Gresley's epoch-making A4s No 2509 *Silver Link* as originally turned out with short front buffers and recessed draw hook.

Although the aim was to reduce air resistance, it was of vital importance that the exhaust steam and smoke emitted by the chimney be lifted clear of the cab windows when working at high speed with early cut-offs. The horizontal wedge form of front end adopted certainly met these requirements. Tests were carried out at the National Physical Laboratory to determine the comparative head-on wind resistance between an ordinary and streamlined Pacific, also the horsepower required at various speeds to overcome the air resistance. In the extreme case of a train travelling at high speed into a gale, the A4 form showed a saving of 639 HP. On a still day 138 HP were saved at 90 mph, rising to 327 at 120 mph, thus giving a valuable bonus of some 4 lb of coal per mile to the publicity value of streamlining.

A number of modifications to the basic Pacific design were made to ensure freer running and an ample reserve of power for fast uphill working. Although the standard valve gear was fitted, the diameters of the three cylinders were reduced by $\frac{1}{2}$ in but the piston valves increased by one inch. Particular attention was given to the size, shape and surface finish of steam and exhaust passages. Boiler pressure was increased by 30 to 250 psi and the distance between the tubeplates reduced from 19 ft to 17 ft $11\frac{7}{8}$ in, allowing the length of the combustion chamber to be increased accordingly.

In order to reduce stopping distances, the brake power was increased from 66 to 93% of the adhesive weight. To ensure good riding qualities and limit the unloading effect in the event of rolling at high speed, the coupled wheel springs were increased in length and flexibility. To equalise wear on the coupled wheel flanges, the initial loading on the bogie control springs was doubled and the inclination of the rear carrying wheel Cartazzi slides altered from 1 in to 7 to 1 in 10.66.

Doncaster works had just six months to build the first A4 which had to be ready for the inauguration of 'The Silver Jubilee' on 30th September 1935. This was achieved with little to spare and the première of No 2509 *Silver Link* is unparalleled in British locomotive history. During a demonstration run on September 27th a seven-coach train was run at an average speed of 100 mph for 43 miles with a maximum of $112\frac{1}{2}$. Delay in the production of further A4s meant that three days later, *Silver Link* had to start working 'The Silver Jubilee' in both directions for a period of three weeks. Involving a daily mileage of 536, including two 230 mile non-stop runs, some 10,000 miles were run during this time of which 7000 were at an average speed of over 70 mph. No mechanical troubles were experienced, proving that Doncaster drawing office and plant works had done their work well; competence in design had been backed by first class workmanship in construction. There were no embarrassing hot boxes or disintegrating inside big ends as occurred with the prototype LMS Pacific, although as is well known such failures were not unknown with the A4s, particularly under wartime and immediate post-war maintenance conditions.

Four locomotives were turned out in silver-grey livery to match the train and given appropriate names with a silver theme. The melodious mellow-toned chime whistle, first used on *Cock o' the North*, was fitted giving the A4s as distinctive a sound as their appearance and performance. *Silver Fox* achieved a new record speed of 113 mph in 1936 whilst working 'The Silver Jubilee', but at the price of an overheated middle big end which did not, however, prevent the locomotive completing the journey to Kings Cross.

A year elapsed before the next batch of A4s appeared, painted in the standard LNER apple green passenger livery. A bird theme was adopted for the names of the new locomotives but there were to be a number of exceptions.

108 The Stanier reply, streamlined 'Princess Coronation' Class 4–6–2 No 6227 *Duchess of Devonshire* passing Edge Hill, Liverpool with an up express. This was one of the red steamliners, built a year or so after the blue 'Coronation' series. (G.H. Soole collection–NRM)

109 Britain's first streamlined high speed train. *Silver Link* heads the 'Silver Jubilee' on a trial run near Hadley Wood, before entering regular service between King's Cross and Newcastle on 30 September 1935.

110 One of the 'Coronation' batch of A4s, No 4492 *Dominion of New Zealand* working the 'Flying Scotsman'.

111 Non-streamlined super Pacific No 2751 *Humorist*. The first Gresley Pacific to receive a Kylchap double blast pipe, a feature subsequently used with such brilliant results on all the Gresley Pacifics.

Following the commercial success of 'The Silver Jubilee' it was not surprising that 1937 saw the introduction of two more high speed trains. The 'Coronation' linked the English and Scottish capitals in six hours and the 'West Riding Limited' London with Leeds and Bradford. Five locomotives were given the names of Commonwealth countries, whilst two, *Golden Fleece* and *Golden Shuttle*, were appropriate to the Yorkshire woollen industry. At the same time the Garter blue livery, later to become standard for the class, was introduced on these locomotives.

In 1937, A3 No 2751 *Humorist* emerged from Doncaster Plant fitted with a Kylchap double blastpipe, followed shortly afterwards by the rebuilt No 10000 with the same arrangement. Up to this time, the high coal consumption of the P2s working in Scotland had not been dissociated from the Kylchap blastpipe, but a close study of the performance of the latest applications resulted in four of the 1938 built A4s being similarly equipped. The first of these, No 4468 *Mallard*, was looked upon as something of a curiosity with its large chimney, thin rasping exhaust and relatively silent running, but soon the whole world was to know of this particular example of the latest development of an already famous class.

112 One of the 1937 batch of A4s under construction at Doncaster Works.

113 *Mallard*, dynamometer car and 'Coronation' train set on 3 July 1938, prior to achieving the world speed record for steam traction.

On the 3rd July 1938, during the course of braking trials with a seven-coach train, *Mallard* achieved a world record maximum speed for steam traction of 126 mph which was never to be beaten. Although not so spectacular in the eyes of the general public, the acceleration from 24 to 74 mph up the 1 in 200 gradient from Grantham to Stoke Box was also a tremendous performance. There is no doubt that a speed of 125 mph was the aim, as prior to the run, the connecting rod stresses at this speed had been carefully calculated and compared with those occurring at 80 mph. It is doubtful if any steam locomotive in the world could have withstood the thrashing meted out to *Mallard* on this occasion without some ill-effect. Possibly resulting from increasing the cut-off from 40 to 45% at 120 mph, the middle big end was found

to be severely overheated after the run, but needing no more attention than the bearing brasses remetalling.

The A4s fitted with Kylchap double blastpipes were without doubt the best of a superb class of 35 locomotives, whether in terms of high speed running, haulage capacity or overall efficiency. Under wartime conditions, No 4901, hauling a 22 coach train weighing 730 tons gross, ran 30 miles on virtually level track at an average speed of over 75 mph. It was the Kylchap A4, rather than a later designed Thompson or Peppercorn Pacific, which was selected to represent the LNER in the 1948 Inter-Change Trials. During these *Seagull* in particular put up some tremendous performances on the Western Region.

When the results were analysed it was found

114 The cab of *Mallard* as now preserved. Typical Gresley features include steam-chest pressure gauge, twin pull-out regulator handles, vertical screw reverse with vacuum lock and GN type firehole door with pivoted trap.

that the overall coal and water consumption of 3.06 and 24.32 lb per drawbar horsepower-hour respectively for the three A4s concerned were the lowest recorded for any locomotive type throughout the entire series of tests. On their homeground, the A4 coal consumption was as low as 2.92 lb per drawbar horsepower hour, whereas the GWR King burned 3.57 lb of Welsh coal and when experimentally fitted with high temperature superheat, could not better 3.10 lb. If proof were needed, there was now no doubt that with the advent of the A4s Doncaster had taken over from Swindon as producer of the most efficient British steam locomotives.

1948 also saw the re-introduction of non-stop working between London and Edinburgh and

115 No 4462 *Great Snipe* is seen here crossing King Edward Bridge over the River Tyne on an up express.
(F.J. Bellwood collection).

116 No 4462 now renamed *William Whitelaw*, at an intermediate stage in the war time removal of the side valances, exposing the driving wheels only.

severe flood damage to the East Coast main line north of Newcastle. This combination of circumstances provided the opportunity for another A4 world record – the non-stop working over a distance of 408.65 miles which was repeated several times with a 13-coach train.

In due course all the A4s (and their A3 predecessors) were fitted with Kylchap double blastpipes with the result that even with the inferior quality coal prevalent in the post-war years, the Gresley Pacifics were more than able to hold their own against the later designs and to deputise for failed diesels. Improvements in workshop overhaul techniques and a minor redesign of the middle big end improved both reliability and mileages between shopping. Significantly, the conjugate valve gear remained unchanged. The famous *Mallard* covered a diesel roster for three weeks, working the down 'Flying Scotsman' to Newcastle, returning to London with the 5 o'clock and running 3216 miles in a week.

That the A4s were still capable of real high-speed running was evident when on 23rd May 1959, the hundredth Gresley Pacific, *Sir Nigel Gresley*, took an eight-coach special train over Stoke summit at 81 mph, attained 112 mph in the return direction, three times reached 100 at widely separated locations running some 25 miles at an average of 100 mph and 55 miles at 90. Two years later, it was a 24 year old A4, rather than a Peppercorn A1 or diesel-electric, which worked the Royal Train to York for the wedding of the Duke of Kent.

With dieselisation of the East Coast main line services virtually complete, the remaining A4s were transferred to Scotland to work the Glasgow–Aberdeen expresses. *Kingfisher* and *Bittern* were the last to be withdrawn from service in September 1966, having outlived their nearest rivals, the LMS Duchesses by some two years.

It is fortunate that, of the six A4s preserved, three of the four still in Britain are in working order, including the record breaking *Mallard* restored to its 1938 condition and displayed in the National Railway Museum.

It is thus still possible, forty years after the emergence of *Silver Link*, to hear the sound of chime whistle and Kylchap exhaust whilst being hauled by an example of Gresley genius.

The Gresley A4 had been in existence for two years before the LMS responded in kind. In fact, the East Coast had made virtually all the running down to the year 1936 and one senses that on the LMS, not everyone was agreed what if anything could be done by way of reply. The LMS was pursuing a policy of a general upgrading of standards and already had a considerably greater total mileage averaging 60 mph or more than any other British company. Undoubtedly, many of the senior staff of the LMS would have preferred not to have to devote time and energy to promoting ultra high speed services with all the special working arrangements that these would need, but the publicity value of Gresley's high speed achievements dominated the whole British scene and the LMS could not stand idly by. Furthermore, it was known that Gresley was

117 A4 No 60033 *Seagull* with side valances completely removed, participating in the 1948 locomotive exchanges at Exeter on the Western Region.
(F.J. Bellwood collection)

planning even more spectacular events for Coronation year in 1937.

By now, Stanier's engines had mostly overcome their initial teething troubles and the Princes type 4-6-2s were turning in haulage and mileage figures fully up to Gresley standards. But there were only 12 of them (plus *Turbomotive*) and there was a need for further 4-6-2s. This was made the excuse for a redesign to incorporate still further improvements. A spectacular trial run of No 6201 *Princess Elizabeth* in 1936 had shown the possibility of a fast London to Glasgow timing in less than 6 hours, but this achievement had been performed by a specially prepared engine. For general day-to-day performance of this nature, something in reserve was necessary. The basic tractive power of the Princess type was adequate but a bigger boiler and some simplification of the front end promised further improvements so Stanier obtained authorisation for a new design of 4-6-2. This was to be known as the Princess Coronation type but later became generally referred to as the Duchess class because of the naming policy adopted for the first batches to be built.

Stanier was away in India for virtually all of the development period for these new locomotives and although his name, as CME, is rightly ascribed to them, most of the design was worked out in detail by Tom Coleman and a fine job resulted. The driving wheels were increased in diameter by three inches to 6ft 9 in, only two sets of valve gear were provided (operating the inside valves by rocking levers) and a bigger boiler was mounted on the new engines. By using nickel steel instead of conventional boiler steel, it was possible to reduce the boiler weight by some two tons and yet still achieve a heating surface somewhat larger than that of the Princess type. In fact, it is quite surprising that an engine so big as the Duchess should in its non-streamlined form weigh only one ton more than the Princess type. In fact, the weight on the coupled axles of the Duchess was slightly less than the comparable weight for the Princess.

Turning now to the internal changes, the whole of the front end of the Duchess class was designed in the Chapelon manner and the new LMS 4-6-2s were clad in a highly spectacular blue streamline casing which basically seemed to have been designed to be as different as possible from that of the A4. As with the A4, the form of the streamline casing itself was something of a subjective affair. It is by no means certain that Stanier himself was bothered about streamlining one way or the other, but Coleman schemed out a casing which was subsequently wind tunnel tested and proved as good as any other shape, so it was retained. In fact it turned out to be a genuine aerodynamic form and better than that of the A4 in that it did not disturb the atmosphere so much. As a natural corollary, this aerodynamic shape made it somewhat inept at lifting the smoke away from the driver's view and in this respect the sloping front of the A4 casing was markedly superior. The LMS does not appear to have claimed any precise figures for horsepower saved by using a streamline casing but its own arrangement probably saved a little more power than did that of the LNER at very high speeds. As a matter of comparison, the weight of a streamlined Duchess was slightly more than five tons above that of the Gresley A4.

The trial run with No 6220 *Coronation* took

118 Stanier 4-6-2 No 6201 *Princess Elizabeth* in its record-breaking 1936 condition with domed boiler–an important step on the way to the Duchess type.

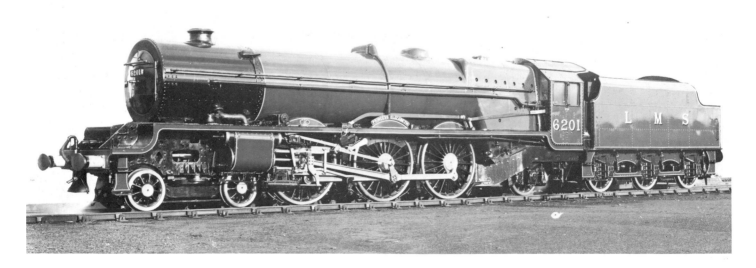

place in June 1937 and, although the LMS had no real racing ground comparable with the East Coast Route down Stoke Bank, a momentary speed of 114 mph was reached on the approach to Crewe, which station was entered over a series of reverse curves at indecent haste at the cost of much broken crockery in the dining cars and a few red faces amongst the high officials. Fortunately, the superb riding of Stanier's locomotive and in particular the De-Glehn type leading bogie, ensured the survival of all concerned and the fact that the train was able to stop at all was no mean achievement. In spite of its exertions, *Coronation* was none the worse for its adventures and was able to make the return trip at sustained high speed, covering the 158 miles from Crewe to Euston in 119 minutes (fully up to modern electric train standards) with no fewer than six maxima in excess of 90 mph yet without exceeding 100 mph – a magnificent piece of controlled high speed running. Over the 67.2 miles from Welton to Wembley, the average speed was 87 mph.

The LMS could, at last, claim the British speed record from the LNER (albeit by a disputed margin) and there can be little real doubt that Gresley's brake trials with *Mallard*, already described, were a convenient excuse for him to put the matter beyond all doubt.

Mallard's speed was never again approached, let alone beaten by steam.

Thus the speed honours eventually rested with Gresley and even had it wished to, which is by no means certain, the LMS Company could not respond in kind, for nowhere on its system could such a speed be safely attempted. Enthusiasts will, doubtless, go on speculating whether or not the LMS design could have gone any faster; for *Coronation* was still accelerating when it had to be slowed down, but this is an area where we refuse to be drawn. Stanier's magnificent engines could claim many superlatives on their own account without any need to speculate.

The first five blue streamlined Duchesses were followed in 1938 by five red streamliners and a further five non-streamlined locomotives for comparison. It was one of this group, No 6234 *Duchess of Abercorn* which, in 1939, was to demonstrate beyond a peradventure, that Stanier's latest design was Britain's most powerful express passenger type. Two tests were carried out, between which the engine was fitted with a simple double chimney and it was with this fitting that the locomotive proved capable of indicating over 3300 HP at the cylinders with a 20 coach test train. The actual drawbar horsepower was regularly between the 1750 and

119 LMS No 6220 *Coronation* under construction at Crew Works, 1937. Note the sloping smokebox top, necessitated by the streamline casings and retained, for a while, when the engine was de-streamlined after the war.

87

2000 mark while the equivalent drawbar horsepower (i.e. compensating for locomotive weight and the effect of the gradient) was at times around the 2600 mark. This sort of performance was well beyond the continuous limit for normal hand firing, but subsequent tests with other engines of the type, not to mention many recorded performances on the road, indicated that this sort of power output was no freak phenomenon. Perhaps the finest of all was the test performance of No 46225 *Duchess of Gloucester* during BR days in 1957 and 1958. These tests, conducted on the ex-Midland Railway Settle to Carlisle line, produced the highest power output ever seen from a steam locomotive in this country. Space precludes all details, but one of the finest of all was a southbound run from Carlisle when, with a

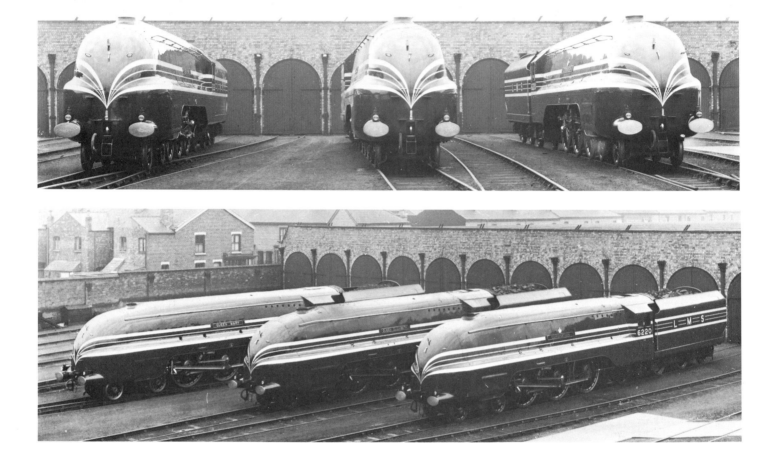

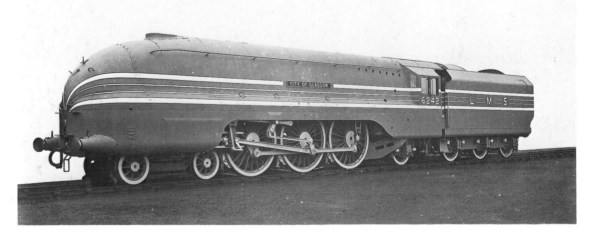

120/121 & 122 Two posed views of the first three blue streamliners – *Coronation, Queen Elizabeth* and *Queen Mary* and a works grey view of one of the final red painted series *City of Glasgow*.

simulated *900*-ton load, the locomotive sustained a steady 30 mph speed on the long and gruelling 1 in 100 climb from Kirkby Stephen to Ais Gill. On this test, coal was being fired at a rate of over 56 lb per minute and the steam rate was 40,000 lb/hr.

As a result of the 1939 tests, all the then existing Duchesses were fitted with double chimneys and all subsequent new locomotives were given them as standard. Few other changes were necessary to the locomotives and they continued in production in limited quantity until the end of the LMS period.

All told, 38 locomotives were built of which the last two embodied a number of additional refinements incorporated by Stanier's successor, H.G. Ivatt, and it was one of this pair, No 6256, which was fittingly named after Stanier himself. The majority of the Duchesses were built streamlined (24 all told), but from 1944, the final examples reverted to non-streamlined configuration and all the streamliners had their casings removed between 1945 and 1949. The whole class then revealed the noble proportions which had, hitherto, only been seen on a few examples. The only other visible changes were the gradual fitting of smoke deflector shields and the replacement of the bevelled top smoke-boxes of the ex-streamliners with a fully cylindrical smokebox during the 1950s. In this form, the class became the mainstay of the heaviest West Coast duties until dieselisation and electrification.

In the 1948 locomotive exchanges, the chosen LMS 4–6–2 No 46236 *City of Bradford* turned out to be something of a disappointment. Although its evaporation rate of 8.67 lb of water per lb of coal was greatly superior to all the competitors it had to take second place to the A4 interms of fuel economy. In fairness, however, it should also be recorded that the LMS 4–6–2 was the only locomotive in the express group to undertake all the assignments whereas the A4 achievement was marred by having to use three separate locomotives because of mechanical problems. During these trials, the Duchesses never managed to better the 'magical' 3 lb of coal per drawbar horsepower figure but they were remarkably economical locomotives, even when worked at maximum capacity. The best

123 The wooden 'jig' on which the complex front curves of the LMS steamliners were fabricated at Crewe.

figure we have seen quoted for a Duchess under high speed conditions is 3.03 lb with the 'Coronation Scot' express while *Duchess of Abercorn* achieved a remarkably low 3.12 lb when putting out its maximum output in the 1939 trials.

As far as we are aware, no front end limit was ever established for the LMS Duchess type and, of course, these formidable outputs could not be sustained over any lengthy period by a single fireman. However, by mortgaging the boiler over a limited period, a keen crew could, in normal service, take advantage of the reserve of power available and there are numerous occasions on record when this was done. In fact, most reliable commentators seem to agree that when called upon to work to reasonably maximum capacity, the general standard of Duchess performance in the immediate pre-diesel period was at a far higher level than in the pre-war years. At the same time, it must be admitted that operating conditions on the London Midland Region during the 1950s sometimes militated against Stanier's big engines, which, sadly for the enthusiast, were not as often called upon to demonstrate their formidable potential as were their East Coast rivals during the same period. This contrast in some respects reflected the different operational conditions on the two sides of the country and merits further mention.

The Eastern Region of British Railways,

124 Front view of LMS streamlined tender showing the steam operated 'coal-pusher', the regulator handle for which is seen in a vertical position to the left of the fire-iron 'tunnel'.

125 Record breaking No 46225 *Duchess of Gloucester*, now fully destreamlined, about to leave Skipton for Carlisle with the LMR dynamometer car and mobile test units on the occasion of the "maximum output" trials, 23rd March 1956.
(W.H. Foster)

largely thanks to Gresley but not forgetting A.H. Peppercorn, had an extensive stock of big 4-6-2 locomotives (not to mention the V2 type) and the loads and schedules could be calculated on the assumption that one of these machines would be available. On the West Coast route, the Duchesses, together with the dozen Princess Royal locomotives, were the only big engines available and therefore they had to work turn and turn about with lower powered locomotives. Although the permitted loads for a 4-6-2 were greater than for the 4-6-0s, it was not uncommon for many loads to be geared to the smaller locomotives, which meant that the big Pacifics were frequently working at less than maximum capacity. Furthermore, on the London Midland Region, the preparations for the electrification of the West Coast route lasted for a long time and severely hampered timetable planning for a lengthy period. This, together with the effects of the gradual replacement of steam by diesel power, had a cumulative effect upon the morale and performance of the drivers and in general it is probably true to say that during the last phase of steam on the West Coast route, the LMS Pacifics did not always show up particularly well by comparison with the ex-LNER locomotives.

The Duchesses and the A4s survived in front line service until the mid.1960s, with the older A4s outliving the final Stanier 4-6-2s by some two years. On average, they enjoyed four more years of service than the Duchesses and received more acclaim, but did not achieve as high a revenue earning mileage figure. This may have been due to the rather harder work which they were often called upon to perform but was more likely the result of there being more high capacity locomotives to share the heaviest East Coast duties. Whatever the precise reasons, only two A4s averaged over 60,000 miles per year

whereas very few Duchesses fell below that figure and the class as a whole averaged some 65,000 miles per year, some 6-7000 miles better than the A4.

On the whole, therefore, if we set aside our prejudices, we must both concede that the honours were just about even between these two fine designs. To those of us who were fortunate in seeing both classes at their best, there were few more exciting sights in the history of British steam locomotives than an A4 in full cry across the plain of York with the Kings Cross-Edinburgh non-stop or a Duchess effortlessly lifting 500 tons or more up Shap or Beattock banks. Although by global standards no more than medium sized locomotives, between them they embody the twentieth century British steam locomotive in its finest form and it seems entirely appropriate that an example of each of them should stand side by side in the British National Railway Museum at York.

126 Rear end modifications as carried out to Nos 46256/7. This picture was taken in 1948 when No 46256 was painted LNWR style lined black and still classified 7P.

127 No 46256 finished its time in BR red livery, very similar to that of the old LMS. This view shows well the superb proportions of all the Stanier 'Duchess' type 4-6-2s when in non-streamlined form. (K. Cooper courtesy-P.B. Whitehouse)

BOILER.

Working pressure, lbs. sq. in.	250	250
Firebox heating surface, sq. ft.	217	230
Tube heating surface, sq. ft.	2,097	2,577
Total	2,314	2,807
Superheater, sq. ft.	653	856
Grate Area, sq. ft.	45	50
Tractive effort, at 85% boiler pressure	40,300 lbs.	40,000 lbs.

Appendix B

Description of the new 4-6-2 streamlined locomotive 'Coronation'

The locomotive in question is one of a new series of five locomotives which will be numbered 6220 to 6224 inclusive. They are being constructed at the Railway Company's Crewe Works and the first engine, No. 6220, named "Coronation" is just completed. The other engines will be named as follows:–

6221 Queen Elizabeth
6222 Queen Mary
6223 Princess Alice
6224 Princess Alexandra

These locomotives are, generally speaking, a development of the earlier 4–6–2 engines of the Princess Royal type, but besides being provided with streamlining have a boiler of considerably greater capacity, while certain improvements have been made to the frames and motion. The tender is also of increased capacity and is fitted with a coal pusher to bring the coal forward to the fireman's shovel when the tender is becoming empty.

The form of streamlining was finally decided upon after very careful experiments with models in the L.M.S. Research Department's wind tunnel at Derby, the test being carried out both to represent head winds and also winds crossing the track at various angles.

The leaving dimensions as compared with the earlier locomotives are as follows:–

	Earlier Locomotives Nos. 6203– 6212.	New Locomotives Nos. 6220– 6224.
4 cylinders, dia. × stroke	16¼"×28"	16½"28"
Valve Gear	4 Sets "Walschaert"	2 Sets "Walschaert"
Travel	7¼"	7¹/₃₂"
Coupled wheels	6'–6" dia.	6'–9" dia.

The appended photograph and diagram show the general appearance and overall dimensions of the new locomotives.

Boiler and Firebox

The boiler shell is constructed of nickel steel, the inner firebox being of copper. The firebox stays are of steel with the exception of the outer top few rows which are of Monel Metal. The throat plate stays are also of Monel Metal.

The firebox is extended into the barrel to form a combustion chamber with the object of allowing the gases to complete their combustion before entering the tubes.

The large flues are screwed into the firebox before being expanded.

Firedoor.

The firedoor is of the sliding type and is carefully designed to direct the incoming secondary air down on to the fire.

Boiler Feed.

An exhaust steam injector with 13 m.m. cones is fitted on the fireman's side, and on the left hand or driver's side is a live steam injector with 13 m.m. cones, both of these are of the flooded type.

Both injectors deliver to the boiler through top feed clack valves which discharge into the trays within the steam space wherein any gases contained in the water may become disengaged, the de-aerated water being finally discharged through pipes below the water level.

Superheater.

There are 40 superheater flue tubes, each containing triple elements 1″ outside diameter, the steam passing to the cylinders is therefore split up into 120 paths.

Regulator.

The regulator is of the grid type and is located in the dome. Baffle plates are provided beneath the dome to prevent water from lifting and entering the steam pipe.

92

Smokebox.

Particular care has been taken in designing the smoke box to so arrange the steam and exhaust pipesthat the smokebox bottom is free as far as possible from all obstructions to facilitate the removal of ashes.

Boiler Mountings.

The boiler is fitted with four Pop safety valves $2\frac{1}{2}''$ diameter. Steam for the various fittings is taken from a manifold on the top of the firebox backplate in the cab. The fittings are of the Company's standard type and it may be mentioned that the carriage warming reducing valve is of increased capacity in order to adequately deal with long trains.

The boiler is provided with a sand gun of the Railway Company's standard type which enables tubes to be cleaned during a run.

Frames.

The main frames are $1\frac{1}{8}''$ thick, and are of high tensile steel.

At each side at the hind end two separate frame plates are spliced to the main frames, and carried through to the hind buffer beam. The outer frames are splayed outwards,and the inner frames inwards to take the side bearers for the trailing two-wheeled truck.

Cylinders and Motion.

There are four cylinders, each $16\frac{1}{2}''$ diameter × 28″ stroke.

The piston valves are 9″ diameter with a maximum travel of $7\frac{1}{32}''$.

There are two sets of Walschaert gear situated outside the frames which drive the outside piston valves direct and the inside piston valves by means of rocking levers, the whole arrangement being specially designed with a view to allowing both sets of valves to be removed for examination with the minimum trouble.

The valve motion is provided with Hoffmann needle bearings except the big ends of the eccentric rods which are fitted with "Skefko" self-aligning ball bearings. The lubrication of the needle bearings is by means of grease gun.

The exhaust passages in the cylinders have been carefully designed to give free exit to the steam without providing an excessive volume which would act as a reservoir.

The exhausts from the inside cylinders and from the two outside cylinders are combined in the saddle casting so that the blast pipe is a simple straight pipe.

The piston valves are designed for lightness and are fitted with six narrow rings to ensure steam tightness.

The pistons are of the box type screwed on to the piston rod and are provided with three narrow rings.

Cylinder Lubrication.

Mechanical lubrication is provided, the oil to the piston valve liners being atomised by being mixed with a jet of saturated steam which is taken from an independent supply on the boiler so that atomised oil is supplied continuously while the engine is running, either with the regulator open or shut.

In addition to the feeds to each of the piston valve liners there are feeds to each piston packing and two feeds to each cylinder barrel, one being at the top and one at the bottom.

Crossheads.

The crossheads are of the two-bar type and are steel castings with bronze slippers having the surfaces which make contact with the slidebars white-metalled. The gudgeon pin is prevented from turning in the crosshead by two keys and is secured by a split cone and nut.

Coupling and Connecting Rods.

The coupling and connecting rods are of "Vibrac" steel, and are designed to withstand the inertia stresses due to high speeds.

Wheel Centres.

The tyres are secured by the Gibson ring type of fastening, and the wheel rims are of triangular section. The balance weights are such that 50% of the reciprocating weights are balanced, equally divided between the coupled wheels. The whole of the revolving parts are balanced in each wheel.

Axleboxes for Coupled Wheels.

These are steel castings with pressed-in brasses completely lined with white-metal on the bearing surface. There are no oil grooves in the crown of the box to disturb the continuity of the oil film, but the oil from the mechanical lubricator is introduced through a row of holes on the horizontal centre line of the axle.

In addition to mechanical lubrication each axlebox underkeep is fitted with an efficient oil pad arranged so that the pad can be easily withdrawn for examination.

A duct shield is also provided on the inside face of each of the intermediate and trailing coupled axleboxes.

The supply of oil from the mechanical lubricator is taken through a spring loaded back pressure valve fixed at the top of the axlebox, the function of which is to keep the oil pipes full of oil while the engine is standing, so that delivery to the journal will commence immediately the engine moves.

The sides of the axleboxes are fitted with bronze slippers, making contact with the faces of the axlebox guides.

Leading Four Wheeled Bogie.

Side bolsters transmit the load from the main frames to the bogie. The bearing springs are of the inverted laminated type with screw adjustment.

Trailing Two Wheeled Truck.

This is of the Bissel type, and the bogie arm is anchored to the engine cross stretcher immediately in front of the firebox throat plate. As in the case of the leading bogie, the weight from the main frames is taken through side bolsters.

Springs and Spring Gear.

All the laminated bearing springs for the engine and tender are made of silico-manganese steel, the plates being of a ribbed section with cotter type of fixing in the buckle.

The spring links are screwed to permit of adjustment.

Rubber damper springs are also provided between the spring link heads and the frame brackets for the coupled wheels.

Brake Gear.

Steam brake is provided, the brake blocks being suitably arranged at the front of each of the coupled wheels. The brake gear is compensated to give equal pressure on each brake block.

The driver's brake valve controls proportionately the application of the steam brake on the engine and the vacuum brake on the train.

Separate steam valves are provided for controlling the steam to the large and small ejectors. A vacuum pump driven from one of the crossheads, is also provided.

Locomotive Cab.

Double sliding windows are fitted on both sides of the cab, and on both sides on the outside of the cab and between the sliding windows a small glass screen can be turned into position so that when the enginemen are looking outside the cab it acts as a draught preventer. A hinged window giving ample area for lookout is fitted on each side in the front cab plate. Tip-up seats are fitted on both sides of the cab and gangway doors are fitted between the engine cab and tender panel plate.

Sanding Gear.

Steam sanding is provided in front of the leading and middle coupled wheels for running in a forward direction, and behind the middle coupled wheels for running backwards.

Oil Gun Lubrication.

Oil gun lubrication is utilised on certain parts, such as the brake gear, spring gear, reversing gear in cab, etc.

Tender.

The tenders carry 10 tons of coal and 4,000 gallons of water and are modified in shape to match the streamlining of the engine and shape of the coaches. As mentioned before, a coal pusher is provided which consists of a steam cylinder mounted on the back of the bunker which can be used to push the coal forward to the fireman's shovel towards the end of the run and thereby save considerable manual effort.

A door is arranged to give access to the coal bunker from the footplate, and on the fireman's side a long receptacle is provided to carry the fire irons.

The tender is provided with water pick-up gear of the Company's standard type fitted with a deflector in front of the scoop to reduce wastage of water.

Oil gun lubrication is also used for such items as the hand brake and water pick-up handles.

E.D. Nº 260A

250 LBS. PER SQ. INCH.

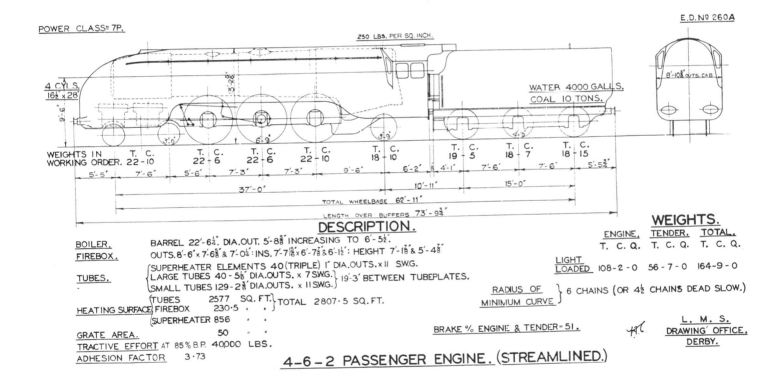

4 CYLS.
16½" x 28"

WATER 4000 GALLS.
COAL 10 TONS.

8'-10⅝" OUTS. CAB

WEIGHTS IN
WORKING ORDER.

T.C. 22-10	T.C. 22-6	T.C. 22-6	T.C. 22-10	T.C. 18-10	T.C. 19-5	T.C. 18-7	T.C. 18-15

5'-5' 7'-6' 5'-6' 7'-3' 7'-3' 9'-6' 6'-2' 8' 4'-1' 7'-6' 7'-6' 5'-5¾'

37'-0'   10'-11'   15'-0'

TOTAL WHEELBASE 62'-11"

LENGTH OVER BUFFERS 73'-9¾"

DESCRIPTION.

BOILER. BARREL 22'-6¼". DIA.OUT. 5'-8⅝" INCREASING TO 6'-5½".
FIREBOX. OUTS. 8'-6"x 7'-6⅝" & 7'-0¼": INS. 7'-7¹⁵⁄₁₆"x6'-7⅞"& 6'-1⅝": HEIGHT 7'-1⅞"& 5'-4⅞"

TUBES. {SUPERHEATER ELEMENTS 40 (TRIPLE) 1" DIA.OUTS.x 11 S.W.G.
{LARGE TUBES 40 - 5⅛" DIA.OUTS. x 7 S.W.G.} 19'-3' BETWEEN TUBEPLATES.
{SMALL TUBES 129 - 2⅜" DIA.OUTS. x 11 S.W.G.

HEATING SURFACE {TUBES 2577 SQ.FT.} TOTAL 2807·5 SQ. FT.
{FIREBOX 230·5 " "
{SUPERHEATER 856 " "

GRATE AREA. 50 " "
TRACTIVE EFFORT AT 85% B.P. 40,000 LBS.
ADHESION FACTOR 3·73

RADIUS OF
MINIMUM CURVE } 6 CHAINS (OR 4½ CHAINS DEAD SLOW.)

BRAKE % ENGINE & TENDER = 51.

WEIGHTS.

	ENGINE.	TENDER.	TOTAL.
	T. C. Q.	T. C. Q.	T. C. Q.
LIGHT			
LOADED	108-2-0	56-7-0	164-9-0

L. M. S.
DRAWING OFFICE.
DERBY.

4-6-2 PASSENGER ENGINE. (STREAMLINED.)

9

An engineering assessment

It would be unrealistic, if not impossible, to make an objective comparison of the achievements of Gresley and Stanier from an engineering or any other viewpoint. Although of the same age and respectively CMEs of the two largest post-grouping railways in Britain, their terms of office only coincided for a period of 9 years, between 1932 and 1941. Gresley had already been a CME for over 20 years when Stanier joined the LMS. Even their engineering backgrounds differed. Gresley had gained experience on the LNW, L & Y and GN railways prior to succeeding to his LNER position, whereas Stanier had spent the whole of his pre-CME career on the GWR. With a major portion

of the LNER serving exclusively the industrially depressed area of North East England, it was, if for no other reason, inevitable that the two railway companies concerned would have a somewhat different locomotive policy. Against this background it is only possible to look at how well each of the two great engineers met the needs and constraints of their respective masters. In both cases it is true to say 'very well indeed'.

The LNER was very publicity conscious and Gresley certainly gave them plenty of 'material'. He built the largest, most powerful and fastest locomotives in Britain. The streamlined trains of 1935 to 1937 were the culmination of his career as both locomotive and carriage engineer and were second to none in terms of speed, comfort and appearance. Whatever the needs of the Operating Department, Gresley provided a tool more than capable of doing the job.

Often the subject of criticism for having three cylinders with conjugate valve gear,when other engineers preferred two or four-cylinder arrangements, Gresley locomotives were nevertheless capable and economical 'work-horses' as well as being 'record-breakers'. In the V2 class of 1936 all the best Gresley features were utilised to produce what was almost certainly the finest heavy mixed-traffic locomotive ever built in Britain. Unlike some CMEs, Gresley took a keen, active and detailed interest in locomotive and carriage design. An inventor in his own right and the holder of several patents, he was continually searching for means to improve the performance and low overall efficiency of the basic Stephenson type locomotive. His adoption of ideas originating at Swindon, in France, Germany and America are examples of his awareness of worldwide developments in the fields of both locomotive and general engineering. He continued to build locomotives to designs other than his own for a number of years after the grouping, and subsequently improved the performance of others by a process of judicious modernisation and rebuilding. Considerable progress was made in standardisation of components, if not (by LMS standards) in locomotive types. Even so, the building of 1518 new locomotives (1153 to Gresley designs) enabled 2393 older ones to be withdrawn up to the end of 1941 and the number of classes reduced from 236 to 164.

It is to him that the major credit for the eventual provision of the modern locomotive testing facilities at Rugby is also due.

128 Centre of gravity tests being carried out on A3 Pacific No 2598 *Blenheim* at Doncaster Plant Works in 1936.

129 & 130 Rivals for the title of Britain's most modern Atlantic–ex-NER Raven three-cylinder 'Z' Class as rebuilt by Gresley in 1933 with Lenz rotary Cam Poppet valve gear and Woodard patent outside connecting rods, and the Ivatt GNR large boiler version as rebuilt a second time in 1938 with two K2 type cylinders and outside Walschaerts valve gear.

131 The LNER under Gresley pioneered the use of electric welding in the construction of locomotives, carriages and wagons. Photographed under construction in Gorton Works is the welded steel firebox with thermic syphon for the second V4 No 3402.

132 Close up of twin articulated 'Coronation' unit showing centre bogie with RH body lifted clear. The folded back fairing on the LH body normally covered the gap between the two.

133 Third class luxury accommodation on 'The West Riding Limited'.

134 The LNER standard 20 goods brake van. Introduced in 1929 it was subsequently adopted as the BR standard.

Gresley took more than passing interest in diesel and electric traction. In the early 1930s he personally attended a demonstration of a diesel-electric shunter and sampled both the German 'Flying Hamburger' and French Bugatti railcars. During the same period the LNER put into service three diesel-electric railcars and a diesel rail-bus. He was involved in two major electrification schemes and the design of the new multiple-unit stock for the North Tyneside lines. His prototype 1500 volt DC 1870 HP Bo-Bo electric locomotive No 6701 became the standard traction unit for Britain's first main-line electrification scheme.

Many of the carriage and wagon design features introduced by Gresley are to be found in vehicles still being operated and built today. Had he never ventured into the locomotive world, there would still be an honoured place for him in rolling stock engineering circles.

O.V.S. Bulleid, who probably knew Gresley as an engineer better than anyone else, wrote of him thus: 'He was incapable of ill-temper, but what I appreciated most was his wide interest in all engineering. He was always ready to adopt any suggestions, but only after consideration. It could be felt that if he agreed to try anything it would almost certainly be a success. He had a

135 Twin-articulated EMU introduced 1937 for the North Tyneside loop services from Newcastle to the coast.

136 Prototype 1500V DC mixed traffic locomotive for the first British mainline electrification scheme. Built in 1941, No 6701 saw considerable service in Holland before taking up the duties for which designed.

wonderful memory, was extremely observant and amongst other things could read a drawing in a way given to few'. A fitting epitaph indeed.

Stanier had a somewhat less adventurous approach to locomotive design and appears to have been content to leave much of the detail work to his Chief Draughtsman. He was not an inventor or the holder of any patents, but he put the Stanier stamp unmistakeably on all future designs of steam locomotive for both the LMS and BR. If Gresley can be criticised for his adherence to the three-cylinder arrangement with conjugate valve gear, so can Stanier, at least in his early LMS days, for the slavish adoption of GWR practices. In all fairness though, it must be remembered that Stanier had

137 In addition to the design, manufacture and repair of locomotives and rolling stock, the CME was also responsible for plant and machinery. D49 No 322 *Huntingdonshire*, fitted with Lenz oscillating Cam Poppet valve gear stands under the huge Mitchell wagon hoist coaling plant at York Depot.

spent over 40 years on the GWR, had no practical experience of any other railway and Swindon was after all in the forefront of British locomotive practice during the Churchward era.

Unlike Gresley on the GNR, Stanier made a somewhat shaky start to his career as a CME, and his future with the LMS was said to have been in real jeopardy following the poor perrformance of some of his earliest designs, particularly the 5XPs. It is a measure of the strength of character and sound engineering knowledge of the man that he was able to overcome these early set-backs and eventually emerge as Britain's leading authority on steam locomotive engineering - an undisputed position after Gresley's death in 1941.

Once Stanier had broken away from the low superheat and smoke box regulator traditions of Swindon, he produced for the LMS locomotives which became renowned for their overall competence and ease of maintenance. In the 8F 2-8-0 he produced a most worthy modern successor to the Robinson ROD locomotives, both of which saw widespread service overseas as well as on 'foreign' railways in Britain. The class 5 4-6-0 was a true 'maid of all work' except for the very heaviest duties and was to be found at work throughout the length and breadth of the largest railway in Britain. Although somewhat overshadowed in the eyes of the general public by their perhaps more glamorous LNER rivals, the Duchesses ran high annual mileages working heavy passenger trains over the West Coast main line in the competent,

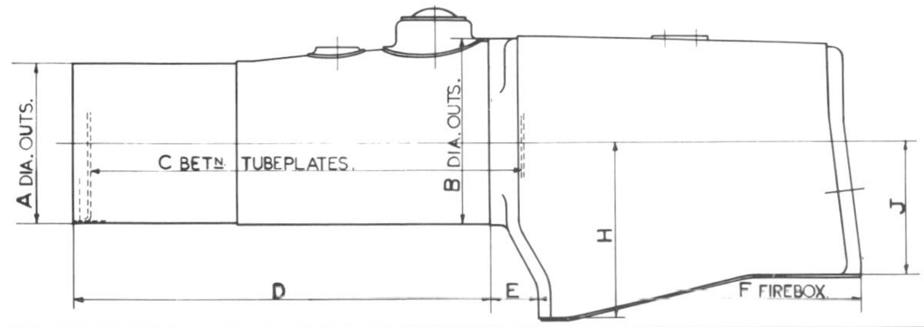

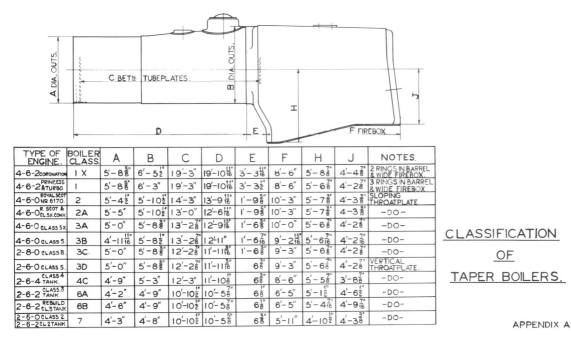

TYPE OF ENGINE.	BOILER CLASS.	A	B	C	D	E	F	H	J	NOTES.
4-6-2 CORONATION	1 X	5'-8 5/8"	6'-5 1/2"	19'-3"	19'-10 11/16"	3'-3 11/16"	8'-6"	5'-8 7/8"	4'-4 7/8"	2 RINGS IN BARREL & WIDE FIREBOX.
4-6-2 PRINCESS & TURBO.	1	5'-8 5/8"	6'-3"	19'-3"	19'-10 11/16"	3'-3 1/2"	8'-6"	5'-6 7/8"	4'-2 7/8"	3 RINGS IN BARREL & WIDE FIREBOX.
4-6-0 ROYAL SCOT No. 6170.	2	5'-4 1/2"	5'-10 1/2"	14'-3"	13'-9 11/16"	1'-9 5/8"	10'-3"	5'-7 3/8"	4'-3 3/8"	SLOPING THROATPLATE.
4-6-0 R. SCOT & CL. 5X. CONV.	2A	5'-5"	5'-10 1/2"	13'-0"	12'-6 11/16"	1'-9 5/8"	10'-3"	5'-7 3/8"	4-3 3/8"	-DO-
4-6-0 CLASS 5X.	3A	5'-0"	5'-8 3/8"	13'-2 7/8"	12'-9 15/16"	1'-6 3/8"	10'-0"	5'-6 7/8"	4'-2 7/8"	-DO-
4-6-0 CLASS 5.	3B	4'-11 11/16"	5'-8 1/2"	13'-2 7/8"	12'-11"	1'-6 7/16"	9'-2 13/16"	5'-6 7/16"	4'-2 7/16"	-DO-
2-8-0 CLASS 8.	3C	5'-0"	5'-8 3/8"	12'-2 7/8"	11'-11 3/16"	1'-6 3/8"	9'-3"	5'-6 7/8"	4'-2 7/8"	-DO-
2-6-0 CLASS 5.	3D	5'-0"	5'-8 3/8"	12'-2 7/8"	11'-11 3/16"	6 3/8"	9'-3"	5'-6 7/8"	4'-2 7/8"	VERTICAL THROATPLATE.
2-6-4 CLASS 4 TANK.	4C	4'-9"	5'-3"	12'-3"	11'-10 1/8"	6 3/8"	8'-6"	5'-5 7/8"	3'-8 7/8"	-DO-
2-6-2 CLASS 3 TANK.	6A	4'-2"	4'-9"	10'-10 1/2"	10'-5 7/8"	6 1/8"	6'-5"	5'-1 1/2"	4'-6 1/2"	-DO-
2-6-2 REBUILD CL. 3 TANK	6B	4'-6"	4'-9"	10'-10 1/2"	10'-5 7/8"	6 1/8"	6'-5"	5'-4 7/16"	4'-9 7/16"	-DO-
2-6-0 CLASS 2. / 2-6-2 CL. 2 TANK.	7	4'-3"	4'-8"	10'-10 1/2"	10'-5 5/8"	6 3/8"	5'-11"	4'-10 1/2"	4'-3 3/8"	-DO-

CLASSIFICATION OF TAPER BOILERS.

APPENDIX A.

138 Classification of taper boilers as used on Stanier locomotives.

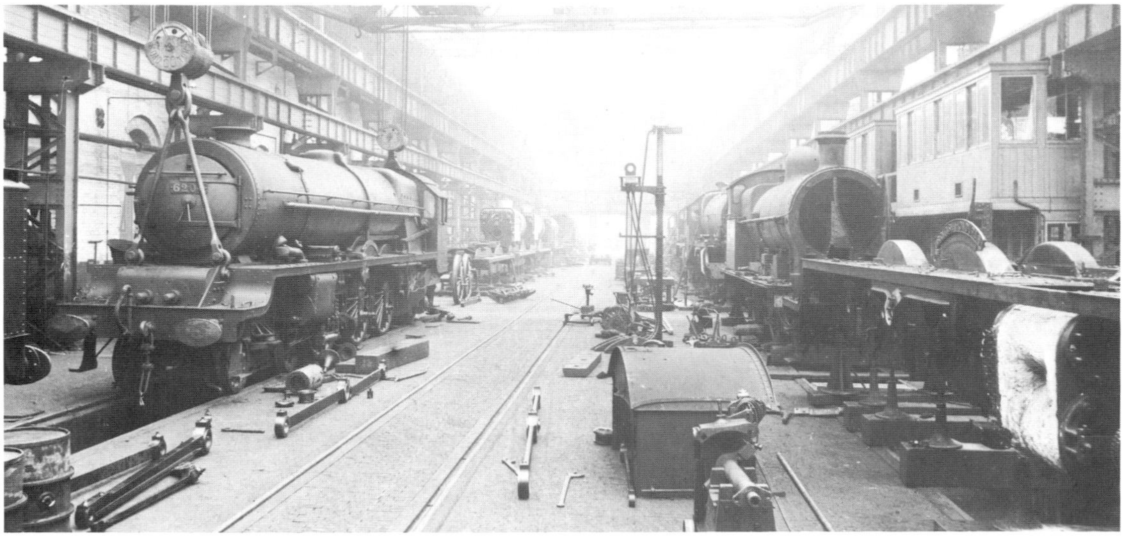

139 The repair shop at Crewe Works showing a preponderance of Stanier types receiving attention, along with a few earlier designs.

if often unspectacular, manner that came to be expected of all the Stanier locomotives.

With ample bearing surfaces and underfeed lubrication, the design of axlebox used on the Stanier classes went a long way to eliminating the curse of hot boxes without recourse to the expense of roller bearings. When later allied to manganese liners it was possible to increase considerably the mileage run between heavy repairs. It is probably true to say that the chemical treatment of boiler feed-water and improvements in axlebox design did more to increase the reliability and availability of steam locomotives than anything else. In the widespread adoption of both these features, Stanier and the LMSR featured prominently.

If his career was somewhat the less spectacular of the two CMEs, Stanier was nevertheless to become a locomotive engineer of the highest stature, much sought after for advice. His work in India as a member of two expert Committees of Enquiry serves as an example of the engineering and general esteem in which he was held. Later, he was to do wartime work as one of three Scientific Advisers to the Ministry of Production.

Both Stanier and Gresley presented papers to the Institution of Mechanical Engineers and each became President of that learned body, thus following in the footsteps of the 'Father of Railways', George Stephenson. As was to be expected, they were also active members of the more specialised Institution of Locomotive Engineers.

They will be remembered as long as railways form a topic of interest and discussion: Gresley, the innovator who designed beautiful carriages and big engines that were world record-breakers and Stanier who restocked the LMS with a fleet of standard locomotives that were to be the major influence in future British railway steam locomotive design.

140 In 1933, No 6152 was taken out of service and extensively modified with Stanier type details–wheels, axleboxes etc, together with a new tender. Repainted externally as 6100 *Royal Scot*, it toured North America with an exhibition train. It is seen here in exhibition finish prior to the tour. Although the exchange of identity remained permanent, the locomotive never ran in service in Britain in the precise configuration shown here.

141 LMS diesel-electric shunter No 7063 built by Armstron Whitworth and embodying jackshaft drive. This was one of the early steps along the way which ultimately led to the familiar BR Class 08 diesel-electric shunting engines.

10

Handsome is as handsome does

It is difficult to find an appropriate note on which to conclude a compilation of this nature. Although we have tried to steer a middle course between the extremes of partisanship which Gresley's and Stanier's designs inspired, we must admit that, in the last analysis, any comparative work may reveal some of the subjective preferences of its authors. We therefore felt it appropriate to finish in an area where both of us are basically in harmony, namely, the appearance of Stanier and Gresley locomotives. These two men on the whole designed very good looking engines.

The steam locomotive is a machine whose basic function usually determines the disposition of its various visible features. Yet it cannot be denied that, down the years, not every designer has managed to blend the functional parts into a harmonious whole. Locomotives need a multiplicity of fittings whose position is fairly well predetermined but whose shape may be schemed out in a far less objective way. Furthermore, one designer's particular preference for one of several possible solutions to a problem (e.g. the form of the firebox) can often impart quite different visual lines to his locomotives. Gresley's and Stanier's designs bore witness to all these considerations and their locomotives were distinctly and differently styled. But both of them generally managed to achieve a good balance of proportion and they did it with classical simplicity of outline and with an absolute minimum of fuss. Their engines usually looked right and their beauty, for that is the right word, was rarely only skin deep.

The visual lines of Gresley's engines evolved rather slowly. He took over from a respected and admired engineer whose locomotives had achieved a high degree of acceptability, so it is not surprising that Gresley's first designs perpetuated many Ivatt features. The cab shape, tender configuration and many other details were carried on with little outward alteration and it was not until the first of Gresley's bigger engines came onto the scene that a distinctively different look began to emerge. The powerful looking K3 and O2 designs, while still in the GNR tradition, were the harbingers of things to come. Particularly pleasing to the eye were the

142 Class H3 No 1640, first of the large boilered Ragtimers, still retaining many of the stylistic features of an earlier age.

143 With his rebuilding of the NER Raven S3 three-cylinder mixed traffic 4–6–0, the Gresley front end and high running plate gave B16/2 No 2364 a modern but pleasing appearance.

144 Striving for increased efficiency by fitting an ACFI feed-water heater had an adverse effect on the appearance of A1 Pacific No 2576 *The White Knight*. (Rev. A.C. Cawston collection–NRM)

145 Wartime black livery and the reverser in back gear cannot disguise the beautifully proportioned and clean lines of the super efficient V2.

details of the front end. The straight outside steam pipes gave a suitably purposeful look to the smokebox area, and the subtle curves of the footplate from front buffer beam to the wholly exposed driving wheels effectively combined the graceful appearance of earlier times with the functional necessities of more modern operating in a way which the K1s, K2s, and O1s, of more patent Ivatt appearance, did not quite manage to do.

Furthermore, with the introduction of his three-cylinder engines, Gresley incorporated some subtle changes in the appearance of the outside valvegear. Most noticeable was the introduction of the three-bar slidebar. This was less conspicuous than the conventional Ivatt twin slidebar and crosshead arrangement and when combined with the lighter rod sections made possible by Gresley's introduction of nickel-chrome steel, produced a beautifully balanced yet totally functional arrangement of the working parts.

The next stage was the replacement of the Ivatt style cab with a rather more substantial twin window design. The GNR type cab looked reasonably well on smaller engines but tended to look distinctly puny when married to the larger Gresley boiler of the K3. All these slight changes were brought together in his first 4–6–2 design and these were the first locomotives on which Gresley also incorporated a taper boiler. Unlike Churchward, Gresley combined his taper boiler with a wide *round topped* firebox which enabled the smooth lines of the top of the boiler to run continuously from smokebox to cab. The tender still perpetuated the GNR shape but was made

considerably larger to match the enlarged size of the engine and a beautifully proportioned ensemble resulted. No matter what the nature of subsequent alterations to Gresley's pioneer 4–6–2s, nothing could mar their fine lines. Later changes, such as the reduced height cab and chimney, the banjo steam collector and high-sided tender gave them, if anything, an even more sleek appearance. Even the addition of double chimneys and aggressively Teutonic smoke deflectors in their final days only served to impart a more pugnacious look to the front end–it could not destroy their classic looks which, for sheer grace and elegance, have in our view no equals in twentieth century British locomotive design.

Stanier's engines, on the other hand, were distinctly different from their LMS predecessors for reasons discussed elsewhere. If Gresley's hallmark was the appearance of the front end of his engines, then Stanier's was probably the taper boiler and Belpaire firebox, features brought with him from Swindon. These had no precursors on the LMS and when applied, as in most cases they were, to a chassis which, visually at least, owed as much to Derby as to Swindon, a totally new look emerged. Technically, the taper boiler is not perhaps quite as valuable on smaller engines as on the larger machines, but in terms of appearance, Stanier's taper boilers suited all the designs to which they were applied.

The blending of a tapered boiler to a trapezoidal firebox is not the easiest of tasks to achieve in visual terms, and early GWR locomotives of this arrangement were not wholly successful. Indeed, some of them caused

146 The characteristic Stanier 'look' is well represented by this view of an unidentified Class 3 2–6–2T and Class 5 4–6–0 in double harness on the Highland main line c.1952. (G.L. Wilson)

considerable offence to contemporary observers. Furthermore, the Churchward chassis was a particularly massive piece of machinery and at first made little concession to aesthetic opinion. Later GWR clases, such as the Castles and Halls, were a considerable improvement in all respects. It is therefore to Stanier's everlasting credit that, although he tended to favour the more substantial machinery of his GWR mentors, he allowed his design team considerable latitude in the visual lines of his LMS engines–probably more so than Gresley, who generally took a keen personal interest in how his engines appeared.

The first Stanier designs (the 2–6–0s and Princess type 4–6–2s) were probably the least successful of his engines in visual terms. Above the footplate they were quite pleasing but the 2–6–0s always looked a little ungainly round the cylinders and the Princesses were not improved by having a rather over-long chassis with the outside cylinders set back over the rear bogie wheels. One of Stanier's team, Mr E. S. Cox, has recorded elsewhere that Stanier knew what he wanted but could not always visualise it precisely. It is therefore fortunate that in Tom Coleman he had appointed a chief draughtsman with an instinctive flair for interpreting his chief's wishes; for it is to Coleman that we must give much of the credit for the aesthetic

147 The most flattering view of the Princess 4–6–2s was probably the conventional ¾ front aspect, especially when associated with the large, 10 ton tender. No 46207 *Princess Arthur of Connaught* is seen here passing Camden No 5 box with the Mid-Day Scot express. (A.H. McNair)

148 The Stanier 2–6–0 was tolerably good looking from the front end, No 13267 (later 2967) at Rugeley Trent Valley c.1934. (P.S. Kendrick).

character of Stanier's engines.

Analysing Stanier's engines on the grounds of appearance is not simple. Above the footplate they clearly derived from Swindon yet, when given a different and distinctly new shape of chimney, a new cab of patently Horwich inspiration, slightly gentler curve radii at the junction of firebox and boiler (which was devoid of the characteristic Swindon safety valve cover), they had a character all their own. Below the footplate, the arrangement of the outside gear was neat and unobtrusive. If not perhaps as slender as the Gresley arrangement, the valve gear was well proportioned and had none of the massively heavy appearance of some GWR designs, even though there were considerably more visible components.

Finally, the new tender shape, with its incurved upper side panels matching the cab roof profile was a fine piece of styling and undoubtedly contributed to the balanced overall effect of Stanier's tender engine designs. This was nowhere better exemplified than in the Class 5 4-6-0 type-surely one of the cleanest and neatest designs of modern motive power ever built. The important part played by the tender in giving good visual lines was particularly obvious if, as quite often happened, Stanier engines were coupled to earlier pattern tenders, when a somewhat unfortunate visual clash resulted.

In the realm of streamlining, Gresley and Stanier adopted different approaches. We are not sure whether we really like the appearance of streamlined engines, but in their different ways both the A4s and the streamlined

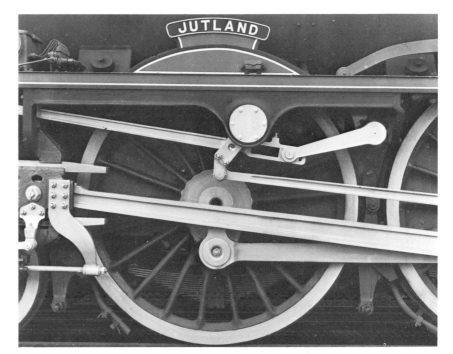

149 Valve gear of Class 5XP No 5684 *Jutland*.

150 This view shows the excellent visual balance imparted by the Stanier style tender-even though the cab of rebuilt Scot No 46155 *The Lancer* is still the Fowler type. Patricroft 1964. (J.R. Carter)

Duchesses were an undoubted triumph for their respective publicity departments. However, if one must have a streamlined engine then we prefer Gresley's final version of the P2 Class 2-8-2. This combined the functionally effective wedge shaped front with a raised running plate to give a happy compromise. In this respect, the removal of the side valances of the A4s during the War did, in our view, go some way to redress the balance. Even so, we feel that the A4 never quite matched up to the A3 in purely visual terms.

The non-streamlined locomotive has, in general, a more honest appearance than its streamlined counterpart, and when the LMS eventually removed the casings from its streamliners, all the Duchesses displayed the fine proportions which hitherto had been seen only on the few non-streamlined members of the class – and what a superb and imposing outline it was, far superior to the original Princess type.

Here was a design whose lines proclaimed its power potential in much the same way as Gresley's non-streamlined Pacifics suggested their speed capabilities without recourse to any artificial aids. So if we choose our favourites on the grounds of appearance only, then they are these; for if there was never a more elegant and graceful twentieth century British locomotive than the Gresley A3, then there was equally never a more majestic looking design than the Stanier Duchess. And on that we rest our case.

151 Class 5 No 44885 entering the Dundee–Perth main line from the Blairgowrie branch in June 1948 with a royal special conveying the Queen Mother – at that time, of course, HM Queen Mary. (G.L. Wilson)

152 Britain's best looking Streamliner?

153 The ugly stovepipe chimney and sloping smokebox did nothing to improve the aesthetic qualities of 6235 *City of Birmingham* when newly de-streamlined. Fortunately, both defects were later rectified.

154 Gresley elegance. The first Class A3 No 4480 *Enterprise* on the 'Scarborough Flyer'. (Rev. A.C. Cawston collection–NRM)

155 Stanier Majesty–No
6254 *City of Stoke-onTrent.*
(G.L. Wilson)

POSTSCRIPT

Since 1976, when the first edition of "Gresley and Stanier" was published, there have been some substantial additions to the National Collection of Railway Relics based at the National Railway Museum of the two CME's products, particularly on the carriage and wagon side. The biggest influx has been of Royal Train vehicles–three 1908-built Gresleys (two saloons and a baggage brake and escort van) from the East Coast Joint Stock train, and the two LMS saloons built in 1941.

Other notable additions include the last wooden-bodied vehicle in BR revenue earning service, 1937 York built Gresley Buffet Car No 9135 and Stanier Corridor Third Brake No 5987.

On the locomotive front the NRM in 1980 transformed "Duchess of Hamilton" from a static museum exhibit to a working locomotive again. Its Gresley rival "Mallard" was in steam again in 1985, for the first time since being withdrawn in 1963. After a partial boiler re-tube in 1977 "Green Arrow" has performed magnificently on a variety of steam hauled charter trains, being chosen to re-open the scenic Settle and Carlisle line to steam traction in 1978 and also work the inaugural BR sponsored steam train services between York, Harrogate, Leeds and Scarborough.

Stanier Class 5 No 5000, still with the original design of domeless boiler, was loaned to the Severn Valley Railway who restored it to Main Line running condition. Since then it has been a regular performer on the SVR and BR.

On the private railway preservation scene, there are numerous examples of the work of both Gresley and Stanier. The first locomotive built by the LNER, the world famous No 4472 "Flying Scotsman", continues to appear almost everywhere that large steam locomotives are permitted, whilst the hundredth Gresley Pacific and post-war speed record holder, No 4498 "Sir Nigel Gresley", has recently received a new lease of life after a major boiler overhaul.

John Cameron's Scottish-based A4, "Union of South Africa", has recently operated south of the border enabling many more enthusiasts to again see "a streak" in BR green livery. The Gresley Society's N2 No 4744 continues to be one of the most regular performers on the Great Central Railway, whilst D49 No 246 "Morayshire" ventures out onto the Main Line from time to time under SRPS auspices. Lord Garnock's K4 "The Great Marquess",currently having a general repair at the SVR's Bridgnorth Works, may well be seen operating again on the line for which designed in the near future.

The Stanier line is even better represented, with the record breaking "Princess Elizabeth" based at Hereford for Main Line operation and sister "Princess Margaret Rose" at the Midland Railway Centre. Most of the major preservation centres have an example of the ubiquitous Class 5 4-6-0 whilst the freight version, the 8F 2-8-0 can be seen working on the WVR and SVR. The magnificent rebuilt Royal Scots can be seen at Bressingham and Dinting, in the form of No 6100 "Royal Scot" and No. 6115 "Scots Guardsman" respectively. "Jubilee" No 5690 "Leander", a regular performer on both the Main Line and SVR, has now been joined by No 5593 "Kolhapur" based at Tyseley as operating examples of the class. The double chimneyed "Bahamas" at Dinting could also soon be running again. In fact with the taper boiler 2-6-0 No. 2968 currently under restoration at Bridgnorth it is still possible to see at least one example of each Stanier basic tender locomotive design for the LMS, if not every variation.

Rolling stock is fortunately also well represented, with the teak-bodied Gresley buffet car being a particular favourite with the operating preserved railways.

It will be apparent from the above that both the serious student of the work of Gresley and Stanier, and the general railway enthusiast, is particularly fortunate in the wealth of examples of the two great engineering geniuses still extant for study and enjoyment.

156 Royal saloon built at Doncaster in 1908 for King Edward VII. On withdrawal from service seventy years later, this magnificent vehicle became part of the National Collection now preserved at York.

157 LMS Royal Saloon No 798 for HM King George VI, built 1941 and wearing its post-1945 LMS livery. The vehicle is preserved in this style.

158 Return to steam for 46229 *Duchess of Hamilton*– leaving York on its first public excursion, 10th May 1980. (M. Welch)

159 The scenic Settle and Carlisle line was re-opened to steam traction in 1978, when Gresley Class V2 No 4771 *Green Arrow* worked "The Norfolkman" over the Easter weekend. The up train on Easter Monday is seen crossing Dent Head Viaduct. (D. Eatwell)

160 Class A3 No 4472 'Flying Scotsman', working a special train on the East Coast main line to celebrate the locomotive's Diamond Jubilee in 1983, is passed at Newark by the latest in High Speed rail traction.

161 The most famous of the six Gresley A4s still extant, the world and post-war steam speed record holders *Mallard* and *Sir Nigel Gresley*, specially posed in 1977 at the National Railway Museum.

113

162 Gresley three cylinder piston valve 4–4–0 *Morayshire* at the Scottish Railway Preservation Society depot at Falkirk in 1981. (T.J. Edgington)

163 Soon to return to traffic on the Severn Valley Railway and possibly on the West Highland Line for which originally designed, Lord Garnock's Class K4 2–6–0 *The Great Marquess* is seen on a Stephenson Locomotive Society special at Worcester. (T.J. Edgington)

164 Preserved No 6201 *Princess Elizabeth* rounding the curve at Miles Platting on 27th September 1980. (M. Welch)

165 Preserved Stanier Class 5 No 5407 on 'Scarborough Spa Express' duty at Falsgrove, 18th August 1981. (BRB)

166 Rebuilt Scot No 6115 *Scots Guardsman* leaves Chinley with a 10-coach test train from Sheffield to Guide Bridge–21st September 1978. (L.W. Goddard)

167 46229 attacking the
Long-Drag at Stainforth
(between Settle and
Ribblehead) on 4th
February 1984. (B.C. Lane)

BIBLIOGRAPHY

E. L. AHRONS *The British Steam Railway Locomotive, Vol.* 1 (London & New York, 1927)

C. J. ALLEN *British Pacific Locomotives*, Ian Allan, 1962

C. J. ALLEN *The Locomotive Exchanges: 1870–1948*, Ian Allan, 1950

F. A. S. BROWN *Nigel Gresley: locomotive engineer*, Ian Allan, 1962

H. A. V. BULLEID *Master Builders of Steam*, Ian Allan, 1963

J. F. CLAY (editor) *Essays in Steam*, Ian Allan, 1970

J. F. CLAY *Jubilees of the LMS*, Ian Allan, 1971

J. F. CLAY *The LNER 2–6–2 and 2–8–2 classes*, Ian Allan, 1973

J. F. CLAY *The Stanier Black Fives*, Ian Allan, 1972

J. F. CLAY and J. CLIFFE *The LNER 4–6–0 classes*, Ian Allan, 1975

E. S. COX *Chronicles of Steam*, Ian Allan, 1967

E. S. COX *Locomotive Panorama, Vol: 1/2* Ian Allan, 1965–6

E. S. COX *Speaking of Steam*, Ian Allan, 1971

D. DOHERTY (editor) *The LMS Duchesses*, Model and Allied Press, Hemel Hempstead, 1972

D. DOHERTY (editor) *Royal Scots of the LMS*, Ian Allan, 1970

B. HARESNAPE *Stanier Locomotives: a pictorial history*, Ian Allan, 1970

Locomotives of the LNER: a multi-volume history (1963): Railway Correspondence and Travel Society

Locomotive Profile Nos 1, 8, 19, 30, 37, Profile Publications, 1970–74

O. S. NOCK *The British Steam Railway Locomotive, Vol. 2* (Ian Allan, 1966)

O. S. NOCK *LMS Steam*, David & Charles, 1971

O. S. NOCK *LNER Steam*, David and Charles, 1969

O. S. NOCK *The Locomotives of Sir Nigel Gresley.* Compiled from articles in *The Railway Magazine*, 1941–3, Longmans, Green & Co 1946

O. S. NOCK *Sir William Stanier: an engineering biography*, Ian Allan, 1964

A. J. Powell *Stanier 4–6–0s at Work*, Ian Allan, 1983

A. J. Powell *Stanier Pacifics at Work*, Ian Allan, 1986

P. N. Townend *East Coast Pacifics at Work*, Ian Allan, 1982

Printed in the UK for Her Majesty's Stationery Office
by W. & J. Linney Ltd.   Dd 736298 C70 9/86